ISBN: 9798390524541

Cover design by: Art Painter
Library of Congress Control Number: 2018675309
Printed in the United States of America

There are a few people whom I would like to acknowledge and give a huge "Thank You"

My late parents Johnny & Bridie, for their love and support and for teaching me the values that have held me in good stead throughout my life.

My late mentor and friend; Philip P. O'Neill, you made me the man that I am today.

My colleagues and friends at The Entrepreneurs Academy whom inspire and influence me every day; especially Joanne Hession, Lorraine Bowen & Suzanne Carroll.

Danielle - watching you grow into the amazing young woman that you have become has taught me so much and you still inspire me to learn more.

Ciara - I love you - this is dedicated to you.

Noel

CONTENTS

PERFECTING THE PERFECT PITCH

For Business

Noel Davidson

"Your work is going to fill a large part of your life, and the only way to be truly satisfied is to do what you believe is great work. And the only way to do great work is to love what you do." - Steve Jobs

CHAPTER 1: THE IMPORTANCE OF A COMPELLING PITCH

Introduction

In today's fast-paced and competitive business environment, capturing the attention of potential investors, clients, or partners is more crucial than ever. A compelling pitch is often the first step towards turning an idea into a successful venture, making it an essential skill for entrepreneurs and business professionals alike. In this chapter, we will explore the importance of a captivating pitch, its role in various business scenarios, and its impact on your career and business growth.

The Purpose of a Pitch

A pitch serves as a concise and persuasive presentation of your business idea, product, or service. Its primary goal is to convince your audience that your offering is worth their time, resources, or investment. A successful pitch can lead to funding, partnerships, and increased brand visibility, while an ineffective one may result in missed opportunities and stagnant growth. The significance of a well-crafted pitch cannot be overstated, as it sets the stage for all future interactions with your target audience.

A. Building Rapport and Establishing Trust

A well-executed pitch not only persuades your audience of your idea's merits but also helps build rapport and establish trust between you and your audience. By presenting a clear, coherent, and engaging pitch, you demonstrate professionalism, credibility, and competence, all of which are vital in fostering strong business relationships.

B. Testing and Refining Your Idea

The process of crafting and delivering a pitch provides you with an opportunity to test and refine your idea. By breaking down your idea into its essential components, you gain a deeper understanding of its strengths, weaknesses, and areas for improvement. Additionally, presenting your pitch to various audiences allows you to gather feedback and insights, which can be invaluable in helping you refine your idea and strategy.

Key Components of a Compelling Pitch

A captivating pitch typically consists of several essential elements, including:

1. Clarity: Communicate your idea, product, or service,

making it easy for the audience to understand its purpose and benefits.
2. Relevance: Demonstrate how your offering solves a problem or meets a need in the market, highlighting its relevance and value to your target audience.
3. Uniqueness: Showcase what sets your offering apart from the competition, emphasising your unique selling proposition (USP).
4. Passion: Express your enthusiasm and commitment to your idea, convincing your audience of your ability to execute and deliver on your promises.
5. Conciseness: Keep your pitch brief and to the point, avoiding unnecessary jargon and information that might dilute your core message.

A. Storytelling

A powerful narrative is often at the heart of the most effective pitches. By weaving your idea into a compelling story, you can engage your audience on an emotional level and make your pitch more memorable. Consider sharing anecdotes, case studies, or personal experiences that demonstrate the value of your idea and illustrate the impact it can have on the lives of your target customers or clients.

B. Emotional Appeal

While presenting logical and rational arguments in your pitch is crucial, incorporating an emotional appeal can significantly enhance its persuasive power. By tapping into your audience's emotions, you can create a sense of urgency, desire, or connection, which can motivate them to take action in support of your idea.

The Role of a Pitch in Business Scenarios

Pitches are essential in various business contexts, such as:

1. Investor Pitches: Secure funding by showcasing the potential return on investment, market opportunity, and strength of your team.
2. Sales Pitches: Attract clients and close deals by presenting the benefits of your product or service, addressing customer pain points and demonstrating your solution's value.
3. Internal Pitches: Influence key decision-makers within your organisation by presenting innovative ideas, process improvements, or new business initiatives.
4. Networking Pitches: Build valuable connections and relationships by quickly and effectively conveying your professional value and areas of expertise.

A. Adapting Your Pitch to Different Audiences

One of the keys to a successful pitch is tailoring your message to resonate with your specific audience. Different stakeholders will have unique interests, concerns, and priorities, and it's essential to address these factors in your pitch. For example, investors may be primarily focused on financial returns, while potential clients might be more interested in the practical benefits of your product or service.

B. The Role of Context in Pitching

The context in which you deliver your pitch can significantly impact its effectiveness. Factors such as the setting, timing, and format of your pitch can all influence how your message is received by your audience. To maximise the impact of your pitch, it's essential to consider these contextual factors and adapt your approach accordingly.

The Impact of a Compelling Pitch on Your Career and Business Growth

A well-executed pitch can have a transformative effect on your career and business. Some of the key benefits include:

1. Funding: By convincing investors of your idea's potential, you can secure the financial support necessary to bring your vision to life.
2. Partnerships: Forming strategic alliances with complementary businesses can lead to mutually beneficial growth and increased market share.
3. Brand Visibility: A compelling pitch can help you stand out in a crowded market, resulting in increased brand recognition and customer loyalty.
4. Career Advancement: Demonstrating your ability to effectively communicate and sell your ideas can open doors to new opportunities and professional growth.

A. Building Confidence and Overcoming Fear

The process of crafting and delivering a pitch can also help you build confidence in your abilities and overcome any fears or anxieties related to public speaking. By repeatedly practising and refining your pitch, you can become more comfortable and self-assured in presenting your ideas, which can have a positive impact on all aspects of your professional life.

B. Continuous Learning and Development

The art of pitching is an ongoing learning process that requires continuous development and improvement. By seeking feedback, analysing your performance, and learning from your experiences, you can refine your skills and become an increasingly persuasive and effective communicator.

Every pitch I have ever coached a participant in has always consisted of five main components. The first component is the opening or the hook, followed by telling your story (past, present, and future), and the final component is making a request for the business.

Beginning with the first main component, the opening or the hook, I would always advise that within the first 30 seconds, one should be able to convey what the product or service does, the problem it solves, how it is different, and why the customer should care.

We use the lean model canvas to describe the first components of this business pitch. For starters, we need to know our audience, our customer segments, and what problems our solutions will solve for them. That is why we begin filling in the lean canvas from the two outer sides of the canvas: the top left-hand corner for the problem and the top right-hand corner for the customer segments.

Starting with the top left-hand corner, list the top three problems that your target customer segments face and briefly describe them. I cannot emphasise enough the importance of these two boxes, as our entire focus during the early stages of a start-up should be on defining and validating these two components. They confirm the existence of the market we are targeting and certify that our solution is relevant to that market. Gather as much data as possible about your preferred customer base and find out what problems they might be facing.

Next, we move to the top right-hand corner to the box marked 'customer segment'. Now that we know what needs solutions, it's time to assess who will use these solutions. Take a close look at the people you had in mind when defining the problems in the previous section. Be very specific when defining customer segments, as you will want to identify your early adopters, who will be your first market, and on whose adoption you will rely. Ensure your segmentation is as detailed as possible.

One suggestion is to give each of your selected demographics a name. For instance, my ideal customer is Susan, aged between 25 and 45, with an average of 2.4 children. She lives in Dublin, Ireland, enjoys watching Desperate Housewives, and has long lunches with her female friends every six to eight weeks.

You may also have another demographic that is an ideal

customer.

For example, my other ideal customer is Jonathan, aged between 35 and 55, recently single or divorced, a Manchester United Football Club fan, drives a seven-year-old German car, and is looking for an opportunity to meet a possible new life partner.

It is crucial at this stage to be as detailed as possible when defining customer segments, as this allows us to target individual customer segments later when defining our route to market.

Next, we move to the middle box to define our unique value proposition, also known as UVP. This is a single, clear, compelling message that states why you are different and worth buying.

Don't worry about perfecting it straight away, as you will need to test it anyway. Create a good enough message that communicates the value your solutions create for your target audience and set up a test environment. Begin testing and see if your audience resonates well with the message.

Your UVP should be a statement of the exact benefit your customer will experience by using your product. Let them know how their situation will improve after you have solved their problem.

One of my favourite books that I use as a reference to explain this concept is 'Start with Why' by Simon Sinek. Simon explains the concept of what our customers go through when making a buying decision. He explains that people don't buy what you do or how you do it; they primarily buy why you do what you do. And this is not based on psychology but rather on biology and how we are made up. There is a part of our brain responsible for all our decision-making, which has no capacity for language. This part of our brain, called the limbic brain, is responsible for all our feelings, like trust and loyalty. It is also the reason why, when faced with all the facts and figures when making a buying decision, sometimes our minds tell us that it just does not feel right. I highly recommend watching Simon Sinek's TED Talk from 2012 on YouTube.

After completing those first three boxes – the problem we solve, who it is for, and our unique value proposition (why the customer should care) – we then move to the next box, which is the second box in from the top left-hand corner, the solution.

The solution is all about how you will solve the problems you found relevant for your target audiences. These can be in the form of a specific product, a set of services, or any combination of the two.

Start by building a minimum viable product (MVP) as your first solution. An MVP is a proxy of the more extensive solution, conveying the core value you can provide and presenting it to your core audience, most likely a group of early adopters. It answers the fundamental questions of your business: what it is about, who it is for, and how it will solve users' needs.

With these four separate boxes filled out, we have the

opening part of our business pitch – the problem, who it is for, and why they should care.

When pitching your business to potential investors, there are six core elements to ensure that your business is investor-ready:

1. Existence of a value proposition: a product or service capability that sets the business apart from the competition.
2. Target market: a clearly defined, reachable, and scalable market for that value proposition.
3. Route(s) to market: feasible paths that can be travelled and within which it is possible to become appropriately visible.
4. Platform for credibility in the marketplace: credibility is at the heart of customer engagement and is essential for effective marketing and sales activity.
5. Team: a team within and around the business (e.g., advisors and/or board level) capable of delivering on the potential.
6. Numbers: financials must make sense to entrepreneurs, investors (public or private sector), and customers.

We will be looking at the Lean Model Canvas in more detail in the next chapter.

As someone who has participated in many pitch competitions as a judge or master of ceremonies, I have gleaned several key learnings from the scoring sheets. The criteria include value proposition, team, target market, financial plan, level of innovation, potential for economic impact, quality of the investor-ready plan, and the actual pitch and interview. Each of these criteria is assigned a score out of 100, with the total being used to evaluate the pitch.

By paying close attention to these criteria and refining your pitch accordingly, you can maximise your chances of success when presenting your business to potential investors. Remember that practice, feedback, and continuous improvement are crucial in crafting a persuasive and impactful pitch.

In summary, perfecting the art of a compelling pitch is an indispensable skill for any entrepreneur or business professional. It is a crucial tool that can significantly impact your career and business's success. By understanding its importance, mastering its key components, and adapting it to various business scenarios, you can unlock a world of opportunities and propel your venture towards growth and prosperity. In the upcoming chapters, we will delve into specific types of pitches, techniques, and strategies to help you craft and deliver pitches that resonate with your target audience and achieve your desired outcomes.

CHAPTER 2: BUILDING A PITCH USING THE LEAN MODEL CANVAS

Introduction

The Lean Model Canvas is a powerful tool to help you create a clear, concise, and compelling pitch for your business. This chapter will guide you through using the Lean Model Canvas to identify and communicate the key elements of your pitch, including the problem your business solves, the demographic of customers who have that problem, your unique value proposition (UVP), and the solution you offer. By following these steps, you'll be able to craft a pitch that is both engaging and persuasive.

Part 1: Understanding the Lean Model Canvas

The Lean Model Canvas is an adaptation of the Business Model Canvas, a strategic tool developed by Alexander Osterwalder and Yves Pigneur. The Lean Model Canvas, created by Ash Maurya, is a one-page visual summary that outlines the core components of a business idea or startup. It's designed to help entrepreneurs quickly and efficiently validate their ideas, reducing the risk and increasing the likelihood of success.

The Lean Model Canvas consists of nine building blocks, each representing a critical aspect of a business:

1. Problem
2. Customer Segments
3. Unique Value Proposition (UVP)
4. Solution
5. Channels
6. Revenue Streams
7. Cost Structure
8. Key Metrics
9. Unfair Advantage

To build a pitch, we'll focus on the first four blocks: Problem, Customer Segments, UVP, and Solution.

Part 2: Identifying the Problem Your Business Solves

To craft a compelling pitch, it's crucial to start by identifying the problem your business aims to solve. This problem should be a genuine pain point or challenge faced by your target customers. By framing your pitch around a problem, you'll be able to engage your audience's empathy and demonstrate the relevance and urgency of your business idea.

To identify the problem, ask yourself the following questions:

- What is the main challenge or pain point your customers face?
- How are your customers currently addressing this problem? What are the limitations of existing solutions?
- What are the consequences of not solving this problem?

Take the time to research and validate the problem you've identified. Speak to potential customers, analyse market data, and study the competition to ensure that you're addressing a real and significant issue.

Part 3: Defining Your Customer Segments

Once you've identified the problem, the next step is to define the demographic of customers who face this challenge. Understanding your target audience will help you tailor your pitch to their needs and preferences, increasing the likelihood of capturing their interest and securing their buy-in.

To define your customer segments, consider the following factors:

- Demographics: age, gender, income, education, occupation, etc.
- Psychographics: values, attitudes, interests, lifestyle, etc.
- Geography: location, urban/rural, climate, etc.

Create a detailed customer persona that represents your target audience. This persona should be based on real data and insights gathered from market research, interviews, and customer feedback. Use this persona to guide your pitch, ensuring that your messaging resonates with your intended audience.

Part 4: Crafting Your Unique Value Proposition (UVP)

Your UVP is a clear and concise statement that communicates the unique benefits your business offers, setting you apart from your competitors. A strong UVP is essential for capturing your audience's attention and convincing them that your solution is worth considering.

To craft your UVP, consider the following questions:

- What sets your solution apart from existing alternatives? What do you do differently or better?
- How does your solution address the problem you've identified in a unique way?
- What are the key benefits your customers will experience by using your solution?

Ensure that your UVP is focused, specific, and customer-centric. Avoid using buzzwords or jargon; instead, use simple and clear language that resonates with your target audience.

Part 5: Presenting Your Solution

The final building block of your pitch is the solution your business offers. This is where you demonstrate how your product or service effectively addresses the problem you've identified, providing tangible benefits to your customers.

When presenting your solution, consider the following:

- Describe the key features and functionalities of your product or service, and how they directly address the problem.

- Showcase the benefits your customers will experience, such as time savings, cost reductions, or increased convenience.
- Provide evidence of your solution's effectiveness, such as customer testimonials, case studies, or data-driven results.

Remember to keep your solution presentation focused and concise, highlighting only the most critical aspects that are relevant to your audience.

Part 6: Bringing It All Together

Now that you have identified the problem, defined your customer segments, crafted your UVP, and presented your solution, it's time to bring it all together to create a compelling pitch.

1. Start by framing the problem in a relatable and engaging way. Use storytelling techniques to evoke empathy and create an emotional connection with your audience.
2. Introduce your target customer persona, highlighting their demographics, psychographics, and the challenges they face.
3. Present your UVP, showcasing the unique benefits your business offers and why it stands out from the competition.
4. Describe your solution, focusing on the key features and benefits that directly address the problem.
5. Wrap up your pitch by summarising the main points and reiterating the value your business

brings to the table.

As you craft your pitch, be sure to practice and refine your delivery, focusing on your body language, voice, and tone. By following the Lean Model Canvas approach, you'll be able to create a pitch that is not only persuasive but also adaptable to different audiences and contexts.

The Lean Model Canvas is a powerful tool for building a pitch that effectively communicates the value of your business idea. By focusing on the problem, customer segments, UVP, and solution, you can create a compelling narrative that captures your audience's attention and persuades them to take action. With practice and refinement, your pitch will become an invaluable asset in your entrepreneurial journey, helping you secure funding, close deals, and influence decision-makers.

Perfecting your Perfect Pitch

PROBLEM	SOLUTION	UNIQUE VALUE PROPOSITION	UNFAIR ADVANTAGE	CUSTOMER SEGMENTS
	KEY METRICS		CHANNELS	
EXISTING ALTERNATIVES		HIGH-LEVEL CONCEPT		EARLY ADOPTERS

COST STRUCTURE	REVENUE STREAMS

CHAPTER 3: KNOWING YOUR AUDIENCE: TAILORING YOUR PITCH TO DIFFERENT STAKEHOLDERS

Introduction

A crucial aspect of crafting a compelling pitch is understanding and addressing the needs, interests, and motivations of your target audience. By tailoring your pitch to resonate with different stakeholders, you increase your chances of effectively persuading them to take the desired action. In this chapter, we will explore the importance of knowing your audience, strategies for conducting audience research, and how to adapt your pitch to various stakeholder groups.

The Importance of Knowing Your Audience

Understanding your audience is essential for creating a pitch that resonates and drives action. By considering their interests, motivations, and concerns, you can tailor your message to address their specific needs and create a more powerful and persuasive pitch.

A. Enhancing Persuasiveness

When you know your audience well, you can craft a pitch that speaks directly to their interests and motivations. This helps you create a more persuasive and engaging pitch, increasing the likelihood of achieving your desired outcome.

B. Building Rapport and Trust

Demonstrating an understanding of your audience's needs and priorities can help you build rapport and establish trust. By addressing their concerns and showing empathy, you signal that you are genuinely interested in their well-being and success, fostering a positive relationship.

C. Reducing Resistance and Overcoming Objections

When you can anticipate and address your audience's concerns and objections, you reduce resistance to your pitch. By proactively addressing these issues, you can increase the chances of winning their support and achieving your desired outcome.

Conducting Audience Research

To tailor your pitch effectively, it's essential to gather information about your target audience. This can be achieved through various research methods, including market research, surveys, interviews, and observation.

A. Market Research

Market research can provide valuable insights into your target audience's demographics, behaviours, and preferences. By analysing market trends, you can identify the needs and priorities of your target stakeholders, allowing you to tailor your pitch accordingly.

B. Surveys and Interviews

Conducting surveys or interviews with members of your target audience can help you gather more detailed and specific information about their interests, motivations, and concerns. This first-hand data can be instrumental in crafting a pitch that resonates with your audience on a personal level.

C. Observation

Observing your target audience in their natural environment can provide valuable insights into their behaviours, preferences, and decision-making processes. This can help you identify potential opportunities or pain points to address in your pitch.

Adapting Your Pitch to Different Stakeholders

Different stakeholder groups will have unique interests, concerns, and priorities, which should be considered when crafting your pitch. In this section, we will discuss various stakeholder groups and how to adapt your pitch to resonate with each of them.

A. Investors

Investors are primarily interested in the potential return on their investment, the strength of your team, and the market opportunity. To tailor your pitch to investors, focus on:

1. Financial Projections: Provide a clear overview of your financial projections, including revenue, profit margins, and growth rates.
2. Market Opportunity: Highlight the size and growth potential of the market you are targeting, demonstrating how your offering addresses an unmet need or demand.
3. Competitive Advantage: Showcase what sets your offering apart from competitors, emphasising your unique selling proposition (USP) and barriers to entry for potential competitors.
4. Management Team: Introduce your team members and their relevant experience, emphasising their ability to execute your business plan and achieve your stated goals.
5. Exit Strategy: Describe your plans for providing a return on investment, such as a potential acquisition, merger, or initial public offering (IPO).

B. Clients and Customers

When pitching to clients and customers, focus on the practical benefits of your product or service and how it can address their pain points. To tailor your pitch to this audience, emphasise:

1. Problem-Solution Fit: Clearly illustrate the problem your offering solves and how it meets the specific needs of your target customers.
2. Features and Benefits: Highlight the key features of your product or service, explaining how they translate into tangible benefits for your customers.
3. Value Proposition: Demonstrate the value your offering provides, including cost savings, improved efficiency, or enhanced customer experience.
4. Testimonials and Case Studies: Share stories of satisfied customers or successful implementations, providing social proof and credibility.
5. Pricing and Payment Options: Outline your pricing structure and available payment options, making it easy for potential clients to understand the costs involved and make a purchasing decision.

C. Strategic Partners

When pitching to potential strategic partners, focus on the synergies between your businesses and the mutual benefits of a partnership. To tailor your pitch to this audience, highlight:

1. Shared Goals and Objectives: Emphasise the common goals and objectives that both parties can

achieve through a partnership.

2. Complementary Offerings: Showcase how your products or services complement those of your potential partner, creating a more comprehensive solution for customers.

3. Joint Marketing and Sales Opportunities: Discuss potential joint marketing and sales efforts, demonstrating how a partnership can result in increased brand visibility and customer reach.

4. Resource Sharing and Cost Savings: Explain how a partnership can lead to shared resources, cost savings, and improved operational efficiency for both parties.

5. Collaboration and Innovation: Describe how working together can lead to new ideas, innovation, and growth opportunities.

D. Internal Stakeholders

When pitching to internal stakeholders, such as colleagues or senior management, focus on the potential benefits to your organisation, as well as the resources and support needed to implement your idea. To tailor your pitch to this audience, emphasise:

1. Strategic Alignment: Demonstrate how your idea aligns with the organisation's mission, vision, and strategic objectives.

2. Business Impact: Quantify the potential impact of your idea on key business metrics, such as revenue, customer satisfaction, or employee engagement.

3. Feasibility and Resource Requirements: Provide an overview of the resources required to implement your

idea, including budget, personnel, and time.

4. Risk Mitigation: Address potential risks and challenges associated with your idea, as well as strategies for mitigating these risks.

5. Implementation Timeline: Outline a realistic timeline for implementing your idea, including milestones and deadlines.

Tips for Adapting Your Pitch to Different Stakeholders

When tailoring your pitch to different stakeholder groups, consider the following tips:

1. Use Audience-Specific Language: Use terminology and language that resonates with your target audience, avoiding jargon or technical terms that may be confusing or alienating.
2. Prioritise Key Points: Prioritise the most relevant and compelling points for each stakeholder group, ensuring that your pitch addresses their specific interests and concerns.
3. Adjust Your Tone and Delivery: Adapt your tone and delivery style to suit the preferences and expectations of your audience, whether it's formal and professional, or more casual and conversational.
4. Leverage Visual Aids: Use visual aids, such as slides or props, to help illustrate your points and keep your audience engaged, ensuring that your visuals are tailored to the needs and preferences of your audience.
5. Address Potential Objections: Anticipate and address potential objections or concerns that may be raised by different stakeholder groups, demonstrating that you have thoroughly considered their needs and priorities.

6. Be Flexible and Adaptable: Be prepared to adjust your pitch on the fly in response to audience reactions, feedback, or questions. This flexibility can help you better connect with your audience and address any concerns they may have.
7. Practice Active Listening: Encourage questions and feedback from your audience, and practice active listening to ensure you fully understand their concerns and can respond effectively.
8. Tell a Story: Incorporate storytelling elements into your pitch to create a more engaging and memorable experience for your audience. Use stories to illustrate your points, share customer experiences, or provide context for your ideas.
9. Show Passion and Enthusiasm: Demonstrating passion and enthusiasm for your idea can be contagious, helping to engage your audience and win their support. Be genuine and authentic in expressing your excitement for your proposal.
10. Maintain Eye Contact and Use Positive Body Language: Maintain eye contact with your audience to build rapport and demonstrate confidence. Use positive body language, such as standing tall and using open gestures, to project confidence and credibility.

Conclusion

Knowing your audience and tailoring your pitch to their needs and interests is essential for crafting a compelling and persuasive pitch. By conducting thorough audience research and adapting your message to resonate with different stakeholder groups, you can significantly increase the effectiveness of your pitch and improve your chances of achieving your desired outcome. As you continue to refine your pitching skills, remember the importance of knowing your audience and the impact it can have on the success of your pitch.

CHAPTER 4: THE ELEVATOR PITCH: MASTERING THE ART OF BREVITY

Introduction

An elevator pitch is a brief, persuasive speech designed to quickly and effectively communicate the essential aspects of your idea, business, or professional background. This concise pitch can be delivered in the span of a short elevator ride, typically 30 seconds to two minutes. In this chapter, we will explore the importance of brevity in pitching, the key components of an effective elevator pitch, and strategies for crafting and delivering a powerful elevator pitch.

The Importance of Brevity in Pitching

Brevity is a crucial aspect of successful pitching, as it demonstrates respect for your audience's time and ensures that you can communicate your message effectively in various situations. The ability to convey your ideas concisely can have a significant impact on your ability to persuade and influence others.

A. Capturing Attention and Sparking Interest

With today's fast-paced and information-saturated environment, capturing your audience's attention is more challenging than ever. A well-crafted elevator pitch allows you to quickly and effectively communicate the essence of your idea, sparking interest and prompting further conversation.

B. Demonstrating Clarity of Thought and Focus

Brevity in pitching demonstrates clarity of thought and focus, as it requires you to distil your message down to its most essential elements. This clarity can help you effectively convey your ideas and increase the likelihood of your audience understanding and remembering your pitch.

C. Adapting to Various Situations and Opportunities

The ability to deliver a concise pitch is a valuable skill in a wide range of professional situations, from networking events and job interviews to sales calls and investor meetings. By mastering the art of brevity, you can be prepared to seize opportunities and make a strong impression, regardless of the context.

Key Components of an Effective Elevator Pitch

An effective elevator pitch should quickly communicate the essential aspects of your idea or business, while also demonstrating your credibility and expertise. The following components are critical for a successful elevator pitch:

A. Introduction and Hook

Begin your pitch with a brief introduction, including your name, title, and organisation (if applicable). Follow this with a compelling hook, which should be a concise statement or question designed to pique your audience's interest and set the stage for the rest of your pitch.

B. Problem Statement

Clearly and concisely articulate the problem your idea or business aims to address. By demonstrating your understanding of the issue, you establish credibility and help your audience connect with your message.

C. Solution and Value Proposition

Present your solution to the problem, focusing on its unique benefits and features. Emphasise the value proposition of your offering, which should explain why your solution is better than existing alternatives and what sets it apart.

D. Target Market and Opportunity

Briefly describe the target market for your solution, highlighting the size and growth potential of the opportunity. This provides context for your idea and helps your audience understand its relevance and potential impact.

E. Proof of Concept and Traction

If applicable, share any proof of concept or traction your idea has achieved, such as customer testimonials, case studies, or key performance indicators (KPIs). This helps demonstrate the viability of your solution and builds credibility.

F. Call to Action

Conclude your pitch with a clear call to action, which should specify the next steps you would like your audience to take, such as scheduling a follow-up meeting, providing feedback, or connecting you with a relevant contact.

Crafting Your Elevator Pitch

To craft a powerful elevator pitch, it's essential to carefully consider and refine each of its key components. The following strategies can help you develop a pitch that effectively communicates your message and resonates with your audience.

A. Define Your Goal

Before crafting your elevator pitch, define the goal or outcome you hope to achieve. This could include generating interest in your idea, securing a meeting with a potential investor, or making a connection at a networking event. By clearly understanding your goal, you can tailor your pitch to effectively address your audience's needs and motivations.

B. Focus on the Essentials

An elevator pitch should convey the most important aspects of your idea or business. To determine these essential elements, consider the following questions:

1. What problem does my idea or business solve?
2. How does my solution address this problem?
3. What makes my solution unique or better than existing alternatives?
4. Who is my target audience, and what is the market opportunity?
5. What proof of concept or traction do I have to support my claims?

C. Be Clear and Concise

Clarity and conciseness are crucial for an effective elevator pitch. Ensure that your message is easy to understand and free of jargon or technical terms that may be confusing to your audience. Additionally, aim to keep your pitch within the recommended 30-second to two-minute time frame.

D. Create a Strong Hook

A compelling hook is essential for capturing your audience's attention and sparking their interest. To create an effective hook, consider using a surprising statistic, thought-provoking question, or bold statement that relates to the problem you are addressing or the value of your solution.

E. Emphasise Your Unique Selling Proposition (USP)

Your USP is what sets your idea or business apart from competitors and makes it uniquely valuable to your target audience. Be sure to emphasise your USP throughout your pitch, highlighting the unique benefits and features of your solution.

F. Develop a Clear Call to Action

A clear call to action is crucial for directing your audience toward the desired outcome. Be specific about the next steps you would like them to take, whether it's scheduling a follow-up meeting, providing feedback, or making an introduction.

Delivering Your Elevator Pitch

Once you have crafted your elevator pitch, it's essential to practice and refine your delivery. The following tips can help you effectively present your pitch and make a strong impression on your audience.

A. Practice, Practice, Practice

Rehearse your elevator pitch frequently to ensure that you can deliver it smoothly and confidently. Practice in front of a mirror, record yourself or enlist friends or colleagues to provide feedback on your delivery.

B. Speak Clearly and Slowly

When delivering your elevator pitch, speak clearly and at a moderate pace to ensure that your audience can easily understand and follow your message. Avoid rushing through your pitch, as this can make it difficult for your audience to absorb the information and may come across as nervous or unprepared.

C. Use Appropriate Tone and Body Language

Adopt a tone and body language that conveys confidence, enthusiasm, and professionalism. Stand tall, maintain eye contact, and use open gestures to engage your audience and project credibility.

D. Be Adaptable and Responsive

Be prepared to adjust your pitch based on your audience's reactions, questions, or feedback. This flexibility can help you better connect with your audience and address any concerns or objections they may have.

E. Engage Your Audience

Encourage questions and feedback from your audience, demonstrating that you value their input and are open to discussion. This can help create a more interactive and engaging experience, increasing the likelihood of achieving your desired outcome.

Conclusion

Mastering the art of brevity in pitching is an invaluable skill that can significantly impact your ability to persuade and influence others. By understanding the importance of brevity, incorporating the key components of an effective elevator pitch, and employing strategies for crafting and delivering a powerful pitch, you can create a compelling and concise message that resonates with your audience.

Remember that practice and refinement are crucial for developing a successful elevator pitch. As you continue to work on your pitch, seek feedback from others and be open to making adjustments based on their input. With dedication and persistence, you can master the art of brevity in pitching and effectively communicate your ideas in any situation.

By honing your elevator pitch, you will not only improve your communication skills but also increase your chances of making meaningful connections and achieving your desired outcomes. Whether you are pitching a new business idea, seeking investment, or networking to expand your professional circle, mastering the art of the elevator pitch is a critical tool for success.

CHAPTER 5: THE INVESTOR PITCH: CAPTURING ATTENTION AND SECURING FUNDING

Introduction

An investor pitch is a vital component of the fundraising process for startups and entrepreneurs, as it allows you to present your business idea, demonstrate its potential, and persuade investors to support your venture. Crafting a compelling investor pitch requires careful planning, in-depth research, and strategic storytelling to showcase the value of your business and convince investors to commit to their resources. In this chapter, we will explore the essential elements of an investor pitch, the process of creating an engaging pitch deck, and tips for effectively delivering your pitch to secure funding.

Understanding the Investor Mindset

Before diving into the components of an investor pitch, it's crucial to understand the mindset and motivations of potential investors. Investors are typically driven by a desire to maximise returns on their investments, while also managing risk. They are looking for business ideas with strong growth potential, solid market opportunities, and a capable team to execute the plan. By addressing these factors in your pitch, you can increase your chances of capturing investor attention and securing funding.

A. Return on Investment

Investors seek opportunities that offer a substantial return on their investment. Be prepared to demonstrate the potential financial returns of your business, including projections of revenue, profits, and valuation growth.

B. Risk Management

While investors are willing to take risks, they also want to mitigate potential losses. Clearly articulate the risks associated with your business and outline your strategies for managing those risks.

C. Growth Potential

Investors are attracted to businesses with significant

growth potential, as this can lead to higher returns on their investments. Showcase the scalability of your business and the size of the market opportunity you are pursuing.

D. Execution Capability

A capable and experienced team is essential for executing your business plan and achieving success. Highlight the strengths and expertise of your team to demonstrate your ability to execute your vision.

Essential Elements of an Investor Pitch

A successful investor pitch should address the key factors that investors consider when evaluating potential investments. The following elements are critical for crafting a compelling pitch that captures attention and secures funding:

A. Problem and Market Opportunity

Clearly define the problem your business aims to solve and the market opportunity it addresses. Provide data and research to support your claims, demonstrating the size and growth potential of the market.

B. Solution and Unique Selling Proposition (USP)

Present your solution to the problem, focusing on its unique benefits and features. Emphasise your USP to illustrate how your business stands out from the competition and why it is uniquely positioned to succeed.

C. Business Model

Outline your business model, explaining how your company plans to generate revenue, achieve profitability, and sustain growth. Be prepared to discuss pricing strategies, customer acquisition, and distribution channels.

D. Traction and Validation

Share any traction or validation your business has achieved, such as customer testimonials, case studies, or key performance indicators (KPIs). This demonstrates the viability of your solution and builds credibility with investors.

E. Marketing and Sales Strategy

Describe your marketing and sales strategies, highlighting how you plan to attract and retain customers, build brand awareness, and drive growth. Provide examples of successful marketing campaigns or sales initiatives, if applicable.

F. Financial Projections

Provide financial projections, including revenue, profit, and cash flow forecasts, to demonstrate the potential financial returns of your business. Be prepared to defend your assumptions and explain how you arrived at your projections.

G. Funding Requirements and Use of Funds

Clearly state the amount of funding you are seeking and how you plan to use the funds. Be specific about how the investment will help you achieve your business goals and generate returns for investors.

H. Exit Strategy

Outline your exit strategy, detailing how investors can expect to realise returns on their investment. This may include options such as an initial public offering (IPO), acquisition, or merger.

I. Team and Advisors

Introduce your team and advisors, emphasising their relevant experience, skills, and accomplishments. Demonstrate how your team is uniquely qualified to execute your business plan and achieve success.

Creating an Engaging Pitch Deck

A pitch deck is a visual presentation that supports your investor pitch, providing a visual representation of the key points and data you are discussing. An effective pitch deck should be concise, visually appealing, and easy to understand. The following tips can help you create an engaging pitch deck that effectively communicates your message:

A. Keep it Simple and Focused

Aim for a pitch deck that is no more than 15-20 slides, focusing on the most important aspects of your business. Avoid overwhelming your audience with excessive information or complex visuals.

B. Use a Consistent Design and Layout

Employ a consistent design and layout throughout your pitch deck, using a clean and professional visual style. This helps create a cohesive and polished presentation that reflects positively on your business.

C. Incorporate Visuals and Data

Use visuals and data to support your claims and make your pitch more engaging. This may include graphs, charts, or infographics that effectively convey complex information in an easily digestible format.

D. Tell a Story

Craft your pitch deck to tell a compelling story that demonstrates the value of your business and the potential for investor success. A well-told story can help create an emotional connection with your audience and make your pitch more memorable.

Delivering Your Investor Pitch

Once you have developed your investor pitch and pitch deck, it's essential to effectively deliver your presentation to engage and persuade your audience. The following tips can help you deliver a powerful investor pitch that captures attention and secures funding:

A. Practice and Rehearse

Rehearse your pitch and pitch deck presentation regularly to ensure that you can deliver it confidently and smoothly. Practice in front of a mirror, record yourself or enlist friends or colleagues to provide feedback on your delivery.

B. Be Passionate and Enthusiastic

Show genuine passion and enthusiasm for your business, as this can be contagious and help create a positive impression on your audience. Investors are more likely to support a business led by a passionate and dedicated entrepreneur.

C. Engage Your Audience

Encourage questions and feedback from your audience, demonstrating that you value their input and are open to discussion. This can help create a more interactive and engaging experience, increasing the likelihood of achieving your desired outcome.

D. Be Prepared to Address Objections and Concerns

Anticipate potential objections or concerns from investors and be prepared to address them confidently and effectively. Demonstrating your ability to handle tough questions can help build credibility and trust with your audience.

E. Maintain Eye Contact and Use Appropriate Body Language

Maintain eye contact with your audience and use

appropriate body language to convey confidence and professionalism. Stand tall, use open gestures, and project your voice to command the room and keep your audience engaged.

Conclusion

Capturing investor attention and securing funding is a critical step in the growth and success of your business. By understanding the investor mindset, incorporating the essential elements of an investor pitch, creating an engaging pitch deck, and effectively delivering your pitch, you can increase your chances of attracting investment and achieving your business goals.
Investing time and effort in crafting a compelling investor pitch can pay off significantly in the long run, helping you secure the resources you need to grow and scale your business. Remember that practice and refinement are crucial for developing a successful pitch, so be prepared

CHAPTER 6: THE SALES PITCH: PERSUADING PROSPECTS AND CLOSING DEALS

Introduction

A sales pitch is a persuasive presentation designed to showcase your product or service, demonstrate its value to potential customers, and ultimately, close deals. Crafting an effective sales pitch requires a deep understanding of your target audience, a clear articulation of your unique selling proposition (USP), and strong communication skills to convey your message and persuade prospects to take action. In this chapter, we will explore the essential elements of a sales pitch, the process of building rapport with prospects, and tips for effectively delivering your pitch to close deals.

Understanding Your Target Audience

Before crafting your sales pitch, it's crucial to understand the needs, motivations, and pain points of your target audience. This knowledge allows you to tailor your pitch to resonate with your prospects and demonstrate the value of your product or service in addressing their specific challenges. Consider the following factors when researching your target audience:

A. Demographics

Gather information on the demographic characteristics of your target audience, such as age, gender, income, and occupation. This can help you create a pitch that resonates with their unique needs and preferences.

B. Pain Points and Challenges

Identify the pain points and challenges that your target audience faces, and consider how your product or service can alleviate these issues. By addressing these pain points, you can demonstrate the value of your offering and persuade prospects to take action.

C. Decision-Making Process

Understand the decision-making process of your target audience, including the factors they consider when evaluating products or services and the key stakeholders involved. This knowledge can help you craft a pitch that addresses their concerns and persuades them to choose your offering.

Essential Elements of a Sales Pitch

An effective sales pitch should address the key factors that influence prospects' decisions and showcase the value of your product or service in meeting their needs. The following elements are critical for crafting a compelling sales pitch that persuades prospects and closes deals:

A. Attention-Grabbing Opening

Start your pitch with a strong opening that captures your audience's attention and sets the stage for the rest of your presentation. This could include a surprising statistic, a thought-provoking question, or a compelling story that relates to your target audience's pain points or challenges.

B. Clearly Defined Problem

Clearly articulate the problem your product or service addresses, ensuring that your audience understands the significance and urgency of the issue. Use data and research to support your claims and demonstrate the impact of the problem on your target audience.

C. Solution and Unique Selling Proposition (USP)

Present your product or service as the solution to the problem, focusing on its unique benefits and features. Emphasise your USP to illustrate how your offering stands out from the competition and why it is the best choice for your prospects.

D. Social Proof and Testimonials

Provide social proof and testimonials to build credibility and demonstrate the value of your product or service. This can include customer reviews, case studies, or endorsements from industry experts, all of which can help persuade prospects to trust your offering.

E. Product Demonstration or Explanation

Show your prospects how your product or service works, either through a live demonstration or a clear explanation of its features and benefits. This allows your audience to see firsthand how your offering can address their specific needs and challenges.

F. Pricing and Value Proposition

Clearly outline your pricing structure and emphasise the value your product or service provides in comparison to its cost. Highlight any discounts, promotions, or special offers that may incentivise prospects to make a purchase.

G. Clear Call to Action

Conclude your pitch with a clear call to action, directing your audience towards the next steps they should take. This could include scheduling a follow-up meeting, signing up for a free trial, or making a purchase. Make it easy for your prospects to take action and move forward in the sales process.

Building Rapport with Prospects

Establishing rapport and building trust with your prospects is essential for successful sales pitching. When your audience feels connected and comfortable with you, they are more likely to be receptive to your message and consider your offering. Consider the following strategies for building rapport with your prospects:

A. Active Listening

Demonstrate a genuine interest in your prospects by actively listening to their concerns, needs, and desires. This not only helps you better understand their unique challenges but also shows that you care about their well-being.

B. Empathy and Understanding

Show empathy and understanding for the challenges your prospects face, validating their feelings and experiences. This helps create a sense of connection and trust, making your prospects more likely to consider your solution.

C. Personalise Your Pitch

Tailor your pitch to the specific needs and preferences of your prospects, using their language and focusing on the aspects of your offering that are most relevant to their situation. This demonstrates your commitment to addressing their unique challenges and can help make your pitch more persuasive.

D. Use Humour and Storytelling

Incorporate humour and storytelling into your pitch, as these techniques can help create an emotional connection with your audience and make your message more memorable. Be sure to keep your humour appropriate for your audience and use stories that relate to your target audience's pain points or challenges.

Delivering Your Sales Pitch

Once you have developed your sales pitch and built rapport with your prospects, it's essential to effectively deliver your presentation to persuade your audience and close deals. The following tips can help you deliver a powerful sales pitch that resonates with your prospects:

A. Practice and Rehearse

Rehearse your sales pitch regularly to ensure that you can deliver it confidently and smoothly. Practice in front of a mirror, record yourself or enlist friends or colleagues to provide feedback on your delivery.

B. Be Passionate and Enthusiastic

Show genuine passion and enthusiasm for your product or service, as this can be contagious and help create a positive impression on your prospects. They are more likely to trust and invest in a solution presented by a passionate and dedicated salesperson.

C. Use Visual Aids

Incorporate visual aids, such as slides or props, to support your pitch and make your message more engaging. Ensure your visual aids are professional, relevant, and easy to understand, enhancing your presentation without detracting from your message.

D. Handle Objections and Concerns

Be prepared to address any objections or concerns your prospects may have, demonstrating your expertise and commitment to finding the best solution for their needs. Handling objections effectively can help build credibility and trust with your prospects.

E. Maintain Eye Contact and Use Appropriate Body Language

Maintain eye contact with your prospects and use appropriate body language to convey confidence and professionalism. Stand tall, use open gestures, and project your voice to command the room and keep your audience engaged.

Mastering the art of the sales pitch is essential for persuading prospects and closing deals, ultimately driving the success of your business. By understanding your target audience, incorporating the essential elements of a sales pitch, building rapport with prospects, and effectively delivering your pitch, you can

increase your chances of closing deals and achieving your sales goals.
Investing time and effort in crafting a compelling sales pitch can pay off significantly in the long run, helping you secure new clients and grow your business. Remember that practice and refinement are crucial for developing a successful pitch, so be prepared to continuously hone your skills and adapt your approach based on feedback and experience.

Adapting Your Sales Pitch for Different Scenarios

Different sales situations may require you to adapt your sales pitch to better suit the specific context and audience. By being flexible and responsive to the unique circumstances of each sales opportunity, you can increase your chances of success. Consider the following scenarios and strategies for adapting your sales pitch accordingly:

A. In-Person vs. Remote Sales Pitches

In-person sales pitches provide the advantage of direct face-to-face interaction, allowing for better rapport-building and non-verbal communication. In these situations, focus on maintaining eye contact, using appropriate body language, and creating a personal connection with your prospect.

Remote sales pitches, such as video conferences or phone calls, require a different approach. Ensure your audio and video quality are clear, maintain vocal energy and enthusiasm, and use visual aids to keep your audience engaged. Additionally, be mindful of time zones and potential technical difficulties that may arise.

B. Group vs. One-on-One Sales Pitches

Group sales pitches may involve presenting to multiple decision-makers or stakeholders. In these situations, it's essential to address the needs and concerns of each individual while maintaining the attention and engagement of the entire group. Consider incorporating interactive elements, such as group exercises or discussions, to keep the audience engaged.

One-on-one sales pitches allow for a more personalised and targeted approach. Focus on understanding the specific needs of your prospect and tailor your pitch to address their unique challenges and concerns.

C. Cold vs. Warm Sales Pitches

Cold sales pitches involve approaching prospects who may have little to no prior knowledge of your product or service. In these situations, focus on quickly establishing rapport, capturing attention, and demonstrating the value of your offering.

Warm sales pitches involve prospects who have already expressed interest or interacted with your company in some way. In these cases, emphasise your understanding of their specific needs and concerns, and build on the existing relationship to close the deal.

Learning from Sales Pitch Successes and Failures

Sales pitching is an ongoing learning process, and it's essential to continually evaluate and refine your approach based on your experiences. By analysing both successful and unsuccessful sales pitches, you can identify areas for improvement and apply lessons learned to future sales situations. Consider the following strategies for learning from sales pitch successes and failures:

A. Debrief After Each Sales Pitch

After each sales pitch, take the time to debrief and reflect on your performance. Consider what went well, what could have been improved, and any feedback you received from your prospect. This process can help you identify areas for improvement and inform your approach for future pitches.

B. Seek Feedback from Prospects and Colleagues

Solicit feedback from prospects, whether you closed the deal or not, to gain valuable insights into your sales pitch's effectiveness. Additionally, seek feedback from colleagues or mentors who can provide constructive criticism and support for improvement.

C. Track Your Sales Pitch Metrics

Track key performance indicators (KPIs) related to your sales pitch, such as close rate, average deal size, and time to close. Analysing these metrics can help you identify trends and patterns in your sales pitch performance and inform your approach moving forward.

By continually learning from your sales pitch successes and failures, you can refine your skills, develop a more effective approach, and ultimately, achieve greater success in closing deals and growing your business.

Sales Pitch Follow-Up Strategies

After delivering your sales pitch, it's essential to have a follow-up strategy in place to maintain momentum and increase your chances of closing the deal. A well-executed follow-up can demonstrate your professionalism, commitment to addressing your prospect's needs, and the value of your offering. Consider the following follow-up strategies to help you turn your sales pitch into a successful business relationship:

A. Send a Thank You Message

Shortly after your sales pitch, send a thank-you message to your prospect, expressing gratitude for their time and attention. This simple gesture can leave a positive impression and help maintain the connection you established during your pitch.

B. Address Any Outstanding Questions or Concerns

If your prospect had questions or concerns during your pitch that you couldn't fully address at the time, be sure to follow up with detailed answers or solutions. This demonstrates your commitment to meeting their needs and can help build trust in your offering.

C. Provide Additional Information or Resources

Share relevant articles, case studies, or other resources that support your sales pitch and help your prospect better understand the value of your product or service. This not only reinforces your message but also positions you as a knowledgeable and helpful resource.

D. Schedule a Follow-Up Meeting or Call

Arrange a follow-up meeting or call with your prospect to further discuss your offering, address any additional concerns, or provide a more in-depth product demonstration. This keeps the sales process moving forward and demonstrates your commitment to helping your prospect find the best solution for their needs.

E. Monitor Prospect Engagement

Keep track of your prospect's engagement with your follow-up communications, such as email opens, clicks, and replies. This can provide valuable insights into their level of interest and help you tailor your follow-up strategy accordingly.

F. Be Persistent, But Respectful

While persistence is key in the sales process, it's essential to balance this with respect for your prospect's time and priorities. Give them space to consider your offering and make a decision, but continue to follow up periodically to maintain your connection and demonstrate your commitment to meeting their needs.

Continuous Improvement and Adaptation

Successful sales pitching is an ongoing process of learning, refining, and adapting your approach based on feedback and experience. As you gain more experience with different prospects, industries, and sales scenarios, you will develop a deeper understanding of what works and what doesn't in your sales pitches.

Continuously seek opportunities for improvement, and be open to experimenting with new techniques and strategies to better connect with your prospects and close deals. By embracing a growth mindset and continually refining your sales pitch skills, you can achieve greater success in your sales efforts and drive the growth of your business.

In conclusion, mastering the art of the sales pitch is an essential skill for anyone involved in selling products or services. By understanding your target audience, incorporating the essential elements of a sales pitch, building rapport with prospects, effectively delivering your pitch, and following up strategically, you can increase your chances of closing deals and achieving your sales goals. Keep learning, experimenting, and refining your approach to sales pitching, and you'll be well on your way to sales success.

CHAPTER 7: THE INTERNAL PITCH: INFLUENCING COLLEAGUES AND DECISION-MAKERS

Introduction

In the world of business, it's not just external clients and customers that require convincing; sometimes, you need to pitch ideas or proposals to your colleagues and decision-makers within your organisation. The internal pitch is a crucial aspect of driving change, gaining support for new initiatives, and fostering a culture of innovation and collaboration. This chapter will explore the intricacies of crafting and delivering internal pitches, focusing on strategies to influence colleagues and decision-makers effectively.

Understanding the Purpose of an Internal Pitch

An internal pitch serves a variety of purposes within an organisation, including:

A. Gaining buy-in for new projects, initiatives, or strategies
B. Securing resources, such as budget or personnel
C. Encouraging collaboration and cross-functional teamwork
D. Driving change and innovation within the organisation
E. Building credibility and showcasing your expertise

Identifying Your Target Audience

Before crafting your internal pitch, it's essential to identify your target audience within the organisation. This will help you tailor your message to their needs, concerns, and motivations. Consider the following categories of internal stakeholders:

A. Decision-Makers: These individuals have the authority to approve or reject your proposal. They may include senior executives, department heads, or other influential leaders within the organisation.

B. Influencers: These stakeholders may not have direct decision-making authority, but they can influence the opinions and decisions of others within the organisation. Examples include subject matter experts, team leaders, or highly respected colleagues.

C. Implementers: These individuals will be responsible for executing the proposed project or initiative if approved. They may include members of your team or other departments who will be directly impacted by the proposal.

D. Beneficiaries: These stakeholders will benefit from the successful implementation of the proposed project or initiative. They may include end-users of a new product or service or other departments that will see improvements in efficiency, collaboration, or performance as a result.

By understanding the needs, concerns, and motivations of each stakeholder group, you can craft a more compelling and persuasive internal pitch.

Crafting Your Internal Pitch

The structure of an internal pitch may vary depending on the specific context and audience. However, several key components should be included to ensure a persuasive and engaging presentation:

A. Problem or Opportunity Statement: Clearly articulate the problem or opportunity that your proposal addresses, demonstrating a deep understanding of the issue and its implications for the organisation.

B. Proposed Solution: Present a well-reasoned and evidence-based solution to the problem or opportunity, explaining how it will address the issue and deliver tangible benefits to the organisation.

C. Benefits and Impact: Highlight the potential benefits and positive impact of your proposal on the organisation, including financial, operational, and strategic outcomes.

D. Implementation Plan: Outline a clear and feasible implementation plan, including timelines, resources, and potential risks or challenges.

E. Success Metrics: Identify the key performance indicators (KPIs) that will be used to measure the success of the proposed project or initiative, demonstrating a commitment to accountability and results.

Tailoring Your Pitch to Different Stakeholders

To maximise the effectiveness of your internal pitch, it's essential to tailor your message to the specific needs, concerns, and motivations of your target audience. Consider the following strategies for adapting your pitch to different stakeholders:

A. Decision-Makers: Focus on the strategic alignment of your proposal with the organisation's goals and priorities, emphasising the potential return on investment (ROI) and long-term value. Present a clear and concise business case, backed by data and evidence, to demonstrate the merits of your proposal.

B. Influencers: Address the specific concerns and interests of influencers within the organisation, highlighting how your proposal can benefit them or their department. Demonstrate your expertise and credibility, and be prepared to provide additional information or resources to support your pitch.

C. Implementers: Speak to the practical aspects of implementing your proposal, ensuring that the necessary resources, support, and training are accounted for. Address any potential challenges or risks and present strategies to mitigate them. Engage implementers in the planning process, seeking their input and feedback to foster a sense of ownership and collaboration.

D. Beneficiaries: Clearly articulate the benefits and positive outcomes that your proposal will deliver for the beneficiaries. Focus on addressing their needs and pain points, and demonstrate how the proposed solution will improve their experience, efficiency, or performance.

Delivering Your Internal Pitch

The delivery of your internal pitch is just as important as the content itself. To maximise your impact and persuasiveness, consider the following best practices for internal pitch delivery:

A. Build Rapport: Establish a connection with your audience from the outset, demonstrating that you understand their needs, concerns, and motivations. Use anecdotes, humour, or personal stories to create a relatable and engaging presentation.

B. Be Clear and Concise: Ensure that your message is

clear, concise, and easy to understand, avoiding jargon or overly technical language. Use visuals and graphics to support your points and make complex concepts more accessible.

C. Be Passionate and Enthusiastic: Convey your passion and enthusiasm for your proposal, demonstrating your belief in its potential to benefit the organisation. Use vocal variety, body language, and eye contact to maintain your audience's attention and engagement.

D. Encourage Participation and Feedback: Invite your audience to ask questions, share their thoughts, or provide feedback during your pitch. This not only fosters a sense of collaboration and openness but also allows you to address any concerns or objections in real time.

E. Be Prepared to Address Objections: Anticipate potential objections or concerns from your audience and be prepared to address them confidently and persuasively. Use data, evidence, and examples to support your arguments and demonstrate the validity of your proposal.

Following Up After Your Internal Pitch

The follow-up process is critical to maintaining momentum and support for your proposal after the initial pitch. Implement the following strategies to ensure a successful follow-up:

A. Send a Thank-You Message: Send a brief thank-you message to your audience, expressing your appreciation for their time and attention. Use this opportunity to provide any additional information or resources that were requested during your pitch.

B. Address Outstanding Questions or Concerns: Follow up on any unanswered questions or unresolved concerns from your pitch, providing detailed answers or solutions to demonstrate your commitment to addressing your audience's needs.

C. Monitor Progress and Provide Updates: Keep your audience informed of any progress or developments related to your proposal, including milestones achieved, challenges encountered, or changes in the project's scope or timeline. This demonstrates your accountability and commitment to the success of the project.

D. Maintain Open Communication: Encourage ongoing dialogue and collaboration with your audience, seeking their input and feedback throughout the implementation process. This not only fosters a sense of ownership and buy-in but also helps to identify and address any potential issues or concerns before they escalate.

Conclusion

Mastering the art of the internal pitch is essential for driving change, innovation, and collaboration within an organisation. By understanding the needs and motivations of your target audience, crafting a persuasive and well-structured pitch, and delivering your message with passion and enthusiasm, you can effectively influence colleagues and decision-makers to support your proposal. By continuously learning from your experiences and refining your approach, you will develop the skills and confidence necessary to successfully pitch ideas and drive positive change within your organisation.

CHAPTER 8: VISUAL AIDS: DESIGNING IMPACTFUL SLIDES AND PITCH DECKS

In today's fast-paced business world, time is a precious commodity. When it comes to pitching your business or idea, you need to capture your audience's attention quickly and keep it for the duration of your presentation. This is where visual aids like slides and pitch decks come in. Visual aids can help you convey complex information clearly and concisely, while also keeping your audience engaged. In this chapter, we will explore the best practices for designing impactful slides and pitch decks that will help you make a lasting impression on your audience.

Understanding the Purpose of Your Visual Aid

The first step in designing impactful slides and pitch decks is understanding the purpose of your visual aid. What do you want your visual aid to achieve? Do you want to provide an overview of your business or idea? Do you want to highlight key features or benefits? Do you want to present data and metrics in a way that is easy to understand? Once you have a clear understanding of the purpose of your visual aid, you can begin to design it in a way that will help you achieve your goals.

Keeping It Simple

One of the most important principles of designing impactful slides and pitch decks is to keep it simple. You don't want to overwhelm your audience with too much information or too many visuals. Instead, focus on the most important points and use visuals to support your message. Use simple language and avoid jargon or technical terms that your audience may not understand.

Choosing the Right Visuals

When it comes to choosing the right visuals for your slides and pitch decks, there are a few things to keep in mind. First, make sure that your visuals are relevant to your message. Don't include visuals just for the sake of having them. Second, use visuals that are easy to understand. Don't use complex diagrams or charts that may confuse your audience. Finally, choose visuals that are visually appealing. Use colours and images that are in line with your brand and that will capture your audience's attention.

Using Consistent Design

Consistency is key when it comes to designing impactful slides and pitch decks. Use the same fonts, colours, and design elements throughout your visual aid to create a cohesive look and feel. This will help your audience stay focused on your message and will make it easier for them to remember your key points.

Using the Rule of Three

The rule of three is a powerful principle of design that can help you create impactful slides and pitch decks. The rule of three states that people tend to remember things better when they are presented in groups of three. When designing your slides and pitch decks, try to group your information into threes. For example, you could present three key benefits, three features, or three data points.

Using White Space

White space is the empty space between design elements on your slides and pitch decks. White space is essential because it helps to create a sense of balance and clarity. It also helps to focus your audience's attention on the most important elements of your visual aid. When designing your slides and pitch decks, make sure to use white space effectively. By the way, white space is not always the colour white ! Choose your background colour of choice but leave space between your design elements.

Using Animation and Transitions

Animation and transitions can be a powerful tools for creating impactful slides and pitch decks. Animation can be used to highlight key points or to draw your audience's attention to a specific element on your slide. Transitions can be used to create a sense of movement or to create a visual break between different sections of your presentation. When using animation and transitions, make sure to use them sparingly and avoid distracting your audience from your message.

Designing impactful slides and pitch decks is an essential skill for entrepreneurs and business professionals. By understanding the purpose of your visual aid, keeping it simple, choosing the right visuals, using consistent design, using the rule of three, using white space effectively, and using animation and transitions wisely, you can create visual aids that will help you capture and hold your audience's attention.

CHAPTER 9: CRAFTING A CAPTIVATING STORY: HUMANISING YOUR BUSINESS IDEA

Introduction

Storytelling is an age-old art form that has the power to captivate, engage, and persuade audiences. In the context of business pitches, crafting a captivating story can help humanise your business idea, making it more relatable and memorable for your audience. This chapter will explore the principles and techniques of effective storytelling in business pitches, focusing on how to create compelling narratives that resonate with your audience and inspire action.

The Power of Storytelling in Business Pitches

Incorporating storytelling into your business pitch offers several key benefits:

A. Emotional Connection: Stories have the unique ability to evoke emotions, helping you create a deeper connection with your audience. By tapping into your audience's emotions, you can make your business idea more memorable and persuasive.

B. Relatability: By humanising your business idea through storytelling, you make it more relatable and accessible to your audience. This can help break down barriers, foster empathy, and increase understanding.

C. Clarity and Simplicity: Stories can simplify complex ideas and concepts, making them easier for your audience to grasp and remember. By using narrative structures, you can present information in a more engaging and digestible format.

D. Differentiation: A compelling story can set your business idea apart from the competition, helping you stand out in a crowded marketplace. By showcasing the unique aspects of your offering through storytelling, you can create a strong and lasting impression on your audience.

Essential Elements of a Captivating Story

To create a captivating story for your business pitch,

you need to incorporate several key elements:

A. Strong Characters: A compelling story is built around strong, relatable characters. In the context of a business pitch, these characters may include yourself, your team members, or your customers. By showcasing the human side of your business, you can foster a deeper connection with your audience.

B. Clear Narrative Arc: A well-structured narrative arc helps guide your audience through your story, maintaining their interest and engagement. The narrative arc typically includes exposition (setting the stage), rising action (building tension), climax (the turning point), falling action (resolving the conflict), and resolution (tying up loose ends).

C. Conflict and Resolution: Conflict is the driving force behind any engaging story, helping to create tension and suspense. In a business pitch, conflict may arise from the challenges your customers face or the obstacles your business has overcome. By demonstrating how your business idea addresses and resolves these conflicts, you can create a compelling and persuasive narrative.

D. Vivid Imagery and Descriptions: Engaging stories use vivid imagery and descriptions to paint a picture in the audience's mind, making the narrative more immersive and memorable. By incorporating sensory details, metaphors, and anecdotes into your pitch, you can bring your story to life and create a more impactful presentation.

Crafting Your Business Story

To craft an engaging and persuasive story for your business pitch, follow these steps:

A. Identify Your Core Message: Begin by determining the core message or theme you want your story to convey. This should align with the overall purpose and goals of your business pitch, providing a clear and consistent narrative thread.

B. Develop Your Characters: Identify the main characters in your story, focusing on their goals, motivations, and challenges. This may include yourself as the founder, your team members, or your customers. Be sure to humanise these characters by providing background information, personal anecdotes, or emotional connections.

C. Establish the Conflict: Define the central conflict in your story, focusing on the problems or challenges your business aims to address. This may include market gaps, customer pain points, or internal struggles within your organisation. By highlighting the conflict, you can create a sense of urgency and demonstrate the need for your business idea.

D. Describe the Journey: Outline the journey your characters go through to address and overcome the conflict. This may involve the development of your product or service, the formation of your team, or the implementation of new strategies within your organisation. By showcasing the obstacles and successes encountered along the way, you can create an engaging and relatable narrative.

E. Present the Resolution: Detail the resolution of the conflict, demonstrating how your business idea has successfully addressed the challenges and improved the lives of your characters. This may include customer testimonials, case studies, or quantitative data to support your claims. By showing the positive impact of your business, you can inspire your audience to take action and support your idea.

Storytelling Techniques for Business Pitches

To enhance your storytelling skills and create a more engaging business pitch, consider incorporating the following techniques:

A. Show, Don't Tell: Instead of simply stating facts or assertions, use vivid descriptions, examples, and anecdotes to illustrate your points. This helps create a more immersive and memorable experience for your audience.

B. Create Emotional Appeal: Tap into the emotions of your audience by using compelling language, evocative imagery, and relatable characters. By eliciting emotions such as empathy, excitement, or even fear, you can create a more powerful and persuasive pitch.

C. Use Metaphors and Analogies: Metaphors and analogies can help simplify complex concepts and make your story more relatable. By comparing your business idea to familiar objects, experiences, or situations, you can help your audience better understand and remember your message.

D. Employ the Rule of Three: The rule of three is a well-known storytelling technique that involves presenting information in groups of three. This can make your pitch more memorable and easier to follow, as our brains are naturally drawn to patterns and groupings.

E. Incorporate Visuals: Use visuals such as images, diagrams, or videos to support your story and make it more engaging. By appealing to multiple senses, you can create a more immersive and memorable experience for your audience.

Delivering Your Story with Impact

The delivery of your story is just as important as the content itself. To maximise the impact and persuasiveness of your business pitch, consider the following best practices for storytelling:

A. Be Authentic: Speak from the heart and share your genuine passion for your business idea. By being true to yourself and your story, you can create a more relatable and engaging experience for your audience.

B. Be Confident: Confidence is crucial for conveying credibility and authority in your pitch. Maintain good posture, make eye contact, and project your voice to demonstrate confidence in your story and your business idea.

C. Use Vocal Variety: Vary your tone, pitch, and pacing

to keep your audience engaged and maintain their attention throughout your pitch. By modulating your voice, you can convey different emotions and create a more dynamic and captivating presentation.

D. Use Strategic Pauses: Pauses can be a powerful storytelling tool, allowing you to emphasise important points, create suspense, or give your audience time to absorb information. Use strategic pauses to enhance the impact of your message and create a more engaging pitch.

Crafting a captivating story is essential for humanising your business idea and creating a memorable and persuasive pitch. By incorporating strong characters, a clear narrative arc, and vivid imagery, you can engage your audience and inspire them to take action in support of your business. By continually refining your storytelling skills and adapting your approach to suit different audiences and contexts, you will develop the ability to captivate and persuade any audience with your business pitch.

CHAPTER 10: THE POWER OF PRACTICE: REHEARSING AND REFINING YOUR PITCH

When it comes to making a pitch or presentation, practice is essential. Practice allows you to refine your message, improve your delivery, and build confidence in your ability to convey your message effectively. In this chapter, we will explore the best practices for rehearsing and refining your pitch to ensure that you deliver a compelling and effective message to your audience.

The Importance of Practice

Practice is essential for delivering an effective pitch or presentation. Practice allows you to:

- Refine your message: Practice allows you to refine your message and ensure that it is clear, concise, and impactful.
- Improve your delivery: Practice allows you to improve your delivery and ensure that your vocal delivery, body language, and nonverbal communication convey confidence and credibility.
- Build confidence: Practice allows you to build confidence in your ability to deliver your message effectively and to handle unexpected situations or challenges that may arise during your presentation.

Best Practices for Practice

To ensure that your practice is effective and helps you to deliver a compelling pitch or presentation, consider the following best practices:

- Practice regularly: Practice regularly to build muscle memory and ensure that you are comfortable with your message and delivery.
- Practice in front of others: Practice in front of friends, colleagues, or family members to get feedback and constructive criticism.
- Record yourself: Record yourself practising your pitch or presentation to evaluate your delivery and identify areas for improvement.
- Focus on your delivery: Focus on your vocal delivery, body language, and nonverbal communication to ensure that you convey confidence and credibility.

- Refine your message: Refine your message to ensure that it is clear, concise, and impactful.
- Prepare for unexpected situations: Prepare for unexpected situations or challenges that may arise during your presentation to ensure that you can handle them effectively.
- Time yourself: Time yourself when practising your pitch or presentation to ensure that you stay within your allotted time and that you don't rush through or omit important information.
- Take breaks: Take breaks between practice sessions to give your voice a rest and recharge your energy.

Tips for Refining Your Pitch

In addition to practising regularly, there are several tips for refining your pitch and ensuring that it is compelling and effective. Consider the following tips:

- Start with a strong opening: Your opening should be attention-grabbing and set the tone for your presentation.
- Focus on your audience: Focus on your audience and their needs to ensure that your message resonates with them.
- Use stories and examples: Use stories and examples to illustrate your message and make it more relatable and memorable.
- Use visuals: Use visuals, such as slides or charts, to reinforce your message and make it easier for your audience to understand.
- Use repetition: Use repetition to reinforce key points and ensure that they stick in your audience's minds.

- End with a call to action: Your closing should be memorable and end with a call to action that inspires your audience to take action.

Practice is essential for delivering an effective pitch or presentation. By practising regularly, focusing on your delivery, refining your message, preparing for unexpected situations, and using tips such as starting with a strong opening, focusing on your audience, using stories and examples, using visuals, using repetition, and ending with a call to action, you can deliver a compelling and effective message to your audience. Remember to practice regularly, seek feedback, and take breaks to ensure that you are refreshed and energised for your presentation. With these best practices and tips, you can refine your pitch and deliver a message that resonates with your audience and achieves your goals.

CHAPTER 11: BUILDING A PITCH LIBRARY: DOCUMENTING SUCCESSES AND LEARNING

Opportunities

Building a pitch library is an essential part of refining and improving your pitching skills. A pitch library is a collection of successful pitches, feedback, and lessons learned that can be used to refine and improve future pitches. In this chapter, we will explore the best practices for building a pitch library and documenting successes and learning opportunities.

Why Build a Pitch Library?

A pitch library serves several purposes, including:

- Documenting successes: A pitch library documents successful pitches and can serve as a source of inspiration and motivation for future pitches.
- Identifying areas for improvement: A pitch library can identify areas for improvement and serve as a source of feedback and constructive criticism for future pitches.
- Refining your message: A pitch library can help you to refine and improve your message by identifying what works and what doesn't.
- Saving time: A pitch library can save time by providing a starting point for future pitches and eliminating the need to start from scratch each time.

Best Practices for Building a Pitch Library

To ensure that your pitch library is effective and useful, consider the following best practices:

- Document successful pitches: Document successful pitches and make notes of what worked well and what didn't.
- Record feedback: Record feedback and constructive criticism from your audience and use it to identify areas for improvement.
- Organise your library: Organise your pitch library in a way that makes it easy to access and search for relevant information.
- Include visuals: Include visuals, such as slides or videos, that were used in successful pitches to provide context and support.
- Update regularly: Update your pitch library regularly to ensure that it remains current and

relevant.

- Include lessons learned: Include lessons learned from each pitch, including what worked well, what didn't, and what you would do differently next time.

Using Your Pitch Library

Once you have built your pitch library, it is important to use it effectively to improve your pitching skills. Consider the following tips for using your pitch library:

- Review regularly: Review your pitch library regularly to refresh your memory and identify areas for improvement.
- Analyse successes and failures: Analyse both successful and unsuccessful pitches to identify patterns and insights into what works and what doesn't.
- Refine your message: Refine your message based on the feedback and lessons learned from your pitch library.
- Share with others: Share your pitch library with colleagues or mentors to gain additional feedback and insights.
- Use as a resource: Use your pitch library as a resource when preparing for future pitches or presentations.

Building a pitch library is an essential part of refining and improving your pitching skills. By documenting successful pitches, recording feedback and constructive criticism, organising your library, including visuals, updating regularly, and including lessons learned, you can build a valuable resource for refining and improving your pitches. Remember to review regularly, analyse successes and failures, refine your message, share with others, and use it as a resource to ensure that your pitch library is effective and useful. With these best practices, you can build a pitch library that supports your ongoing growth and success as a pitcher.

CHAPTER 12: COMMUNICATING YOUR UNIQUE SELLING PROPOSITION (USP)

Introduction

A Unique Selling Proposition (USP) is a crucial element of any business pitch, as it sets your product or service apart from competitors and communicates the specific benefits that customers can expect from your offering. In this chapter, we will explore the process of identifying and communicating your USP effectively, ensuring that your pitch resonates with your target audience and showcases the unique value that your business brings to the market.

Understanding the Unique Selling Proposition (USP)

A USP is a statement that encapsulates the distinct benefits or advantages that your business offers compared to others in the market. It should answer the following questions:

1. What makes your product or service unique?
2. Why should customers choose your offering over others?
3. How does your business solve a specific problem or meet a particular need?

Identifying Your USP

To identify your USP, you will need to conduct thorough research and analysis of both your business and the market landscape. Consider the following steps to help you pinpoint your unique selling points:

1. Analyse Your Offering: Examine the features, benefits, and qualities of your product or service. Identify any aspects that set it apart from competitors, such as innovative technology, superior performance, or a unique approach to solving a problem.

2. Understand Your Target Market: Conduct market research to understand the needs, preferences, and pain points of your target audience. This will help you identify the specific benefits that your offering can provide to this group, such as convenience, cost savings, or improved quality of life.

3. Assess Your Competitors: Analyse your competition to determine their strengths and weaknesses. By understanding how your offering compares to others in the market, you can highlight the unique advantages that set your business apart.

4. Identify Your Differentiators: Based on your research and analysis, pinpoint the specific factors that differentiate your business from competitors. These may include exceptional customer service, a strong brand reputation, or a commitment to sustainability and social responsibility.

Crafting Your USP Statement

Once you have identified your USP, you will need to craft a concise and compelling statement that communicates it clearly and effectively. Consider the following tips for creating an impactful USP statement:

1. Keep It Simple: Your USP statement should be clear and straightforward, avoiding jargon or overly technical language. Aim to distil your USP into a single sentence or phrase that can be easily understood by your target audience.

2. Be Specific: Avoid vague or generic statements that could apply to multiple businesses. Instead, focus on the specific aspects that make your offering unique, such as patented technology, a first-to-market advantage, or a revolutionary approach to addressing a common problem.

3. Focus on Benefits: Emphasise the benefits that customers can expect from your product or service, rather than simply listing its features or capabilities. This will help your audience understand the direct impact that your offering can have on their lives or businesses.

4. Be Memorable: Use vivid and evocative language to create a memorable USP statement that sticks in your audience's mind. This may involve using metaphors, alliteration, or rhetorical devices to make your USP more engaging and impactful.

Communicating Your USP in Your Business Pitch

Incorporating your USP into your business pitch is essential for capturing your audience's attention and differentiating your offering from competitors. Consider the following strategies for effectively communicating your USP:

A. Position Your USP Prominently: Feature your USP prominently in your pitch, ensuring that it is one of the first things your audience hears. This will help establish your unique value proposition from the outset and set the tone for the rest of your presentation.

B. Provide Evidence and Examples: Support your USP statement with concrete evidence and examples that demonstrate the unique benefits of your offering. This may include customer testimonials, case studies, or quantitative data that showcase the impact of your product or service.

C. Address Objections: Anticipate potential objections or concerns that your audience may have about your USP and address them proactively in your pitch. By demonstrating that you have considered potential challenges and have the plan to overcome them, you can build credibility and trust with your audience.

D. Reinforce Your USP Throughout Your Pitch: Consistently refer back to your USP throughout your pitch, linking it to various aspects of your presentation. This will help reinforce the unique value that your business offers and ensure that your USP remains top of mind for your audience.

E. Focus on Relevant Benefits: Highlight the specific benefits that are most relevant to your audience, emphasising the unique value that your offering can provide to them. For example, if pitching to investors, emphasise the market potential and revenue growth opportunities; if pitching to customers, focus on the direct impact your product or service can have on their lives or businesses.

F. Adjust Your Language and Tone: Adapt your language and tone to suit the preferences and expectations of your audience. For example, a pitch to a group of technical experts may require more in-depth explanations and jargon, while a pitch to a general audience should be more accessible and straightforward.

G. Address Audience-Specific Concerns: Identify any

concerns or objections that are unique to your audience and address them proactively in your pitch. By demonstrating that you understand your audience's needs and priorities, you can build rapport and credibility.

Evaluating and Refining Your USP

As your business evolves and the market landscape shifts, it is important to continually evaluate and refine your USP to ensure it remains relevant and compelling. Consider the following strategies for reviewing and updating your USP:

A. Monitor Market Changes: Keep abreast of changes in the market, including new competitors, emerging trends, and evolving customer needs. This will help you identify any adjustments that may be necessary to maintain your unique competitive advantage.

B. Gather Customer Feedback: Solicit feedback from your customers on their experiences with your product or service, as well as their perceptions of your USP. This can provide valuable insights into areas where your USP may need improvement or refinement.

C. Conduct Regular Reviews: Periodically review your USP to ensure it remains accurate and up-to-date, adjusting it as needed to reflect changes in your business or the market. This will help ensure that your USP continues to resonate with your target audience and effectively differentiates your offering from competitors.

Your Unique Selling Proposition is a critical component of your business pitch, helping to set your offering apart from the competition and communicate the specific benefits and advantages that your business provides. By carefully identifying, crafting, and communicating your USP, you can create a compelling and persuasive pitch that resonates with your target audience and showcases the unique value that your business brings to the market. By continually refining and updating your USP in response to changes in your business and the market landscape, you can ensure that your pitch remains relevant and impactful, helping you to stand out in a crowded marketplace and achieve lasting success.

CHAPTER 13: DATA-DRIVEN PITCHES: PRESENTING NUMBERS AND METRICS EFFECTIVELY

In today's business world, data-driven decision-making has become the norm. Companies are collecting and analysing vast amounts of data to make informed decisions about everything from product development to customer acquisition. Therefore, the ability to present data and metrics effectively has become an essential skill for entrepreneurs and business professionals. In this chapter, we will explore the best practices for presenting numbers and metrics in your pitch, including the importance of data visualisation, choosing the right metrics, and telling a compelling story with your data.

The Importance of Data Visualisation

When presenting data and metrics in a pitch, it is essential to remember that not everyone in your audience will be a data expert. Therefore, it is crucial to present your data in a way that is easy to understand and visually appealing. This is where data visualisation comes in. Data visualisation is the process of representing data in a graphical or pictorial format that makes it easier to understand and analyse.

One of the most popular types of data visualisation is the infographic. Infographics combine text, images, and data to tell a compelling story. They are an excellent way to communicate complex information in an easy-to-understand format. When designing an infographic, it is essential to keep in mind your audience and the purpose of your pitch. Choose colours, fonts, and images that align with your brand and your message.

Another popular type of data visualisation is a chart or graph. Charts and graphs are useful for presenting numerical data and comparing different sets of data. There are many types of charts and graphs, including line graphs, bar graphs, pie charts, and scatterplots. When choosing a chart or graph, it is essential to select the one that best represents your data and is easy to read and understand.

Choosing the Right Metrics

When presenting data in a pitch, it is essential to choose the right metrics. Metrics are numerical measurements that help you track progress and performance. The metrics you choose will depend on your business goals and objectives. For example, if your goal is to increase revenue, you might track metrics like sales revenue, profit margin, and customer acquisition cost.

When choosing metrics for your pitch, it is essential to choose ones that are relevant and actionable. Relevant metrics align with your business goals and objectives. Actionable metrics are ones that you can take action on to improve performance. For example, if you are tracking customer acquisition costs, you might take action to reduce advertising spend or improve your conversion rate.

Telling a Compelling Story with Your Data

Presenting data and metrics is not enough. To be effective, you must tell a compelling story with your data. Your story should have a clear beginning, middle, and end, and it should be easy to follow. Here are some tips for telling a compelling story with your data:

1. Start with a hook: Your opening should grab your audience's attention and make them want to learn more.
2. Provide context: Help your audience understand why the data is important and how it relates to your business goals.
3. Use storytelling techniques: Use anecdotes,

examples, and metaphors to make your data more relatable and memorable.

4. Emphasise the most important points: Highlight the key takeaways from your data and explain why they matter.
5. End with a call to action: Encourage your audience to take action based on your data and metrics.

Presenting data and metrics effectively is an essential skill for entrepreneurs and business professionals. To be successful, you must choose the right metrics, present your data in a visually appealing way, and tell a compelling story with your data. By following these best practices, you can make your pitch more persuasive and increase your chances of success. Remember, data is only useful if you can communicate

CHAPTER 14: BODY LANGUAGE AND NONVERBAL COMMUNICATION

Conveying Confidence and Credibility

When it comes to making a pitch or presentation, it's not just what you say that matters, it's also how you say it. Your body language and nonverbal communication can have a significant impact on how your audience perceives you and your message. In this chapter, we will explore the best practices for conveying confidence and credibility through your body language and nonverbal communication.

The Importance of Body Language

Body language is the nonverbal communication that we use to convey meaning and emotion. Body language includes facial expressions, gestures, posture, and eye contact. Studies have shown that body language can account for up to 93% of the communication that takes place in a conversation, with only 7% of communication coming from the words that are spoken.

Body language is important because it can convey emotions and attitudes that are not expressed through words. For example, if you are slouching or avoiding eye contact, your audience may perceive you as disinterested or untrustworthy. Conversely, if you are standing tall with open body language and maintaining eye contact, your audience will perceive you as confident and credible.

Using Open Body Language

One of the most important aspects of body language is the use of open body language. Open body language includes standing or sitting tall with your shoulders back, maintaining eye contact, and using expansive gestures. Open body language conveys confidence and openness, and it can help to build trust with your audience.

When using open body language, it is important to be mindful of your posture. Avoid slouching or crossing your arms or legs, as this can convey defensiveness or disinterest. Instead, stand or sit tall with your shoulders back and your arms at your sides or gesturing naturally.

Maintaining Eye Contact

Maintaining eye contact is another essential aspect

of body language. Eye contact conveys confidence, engagement, and sincerity. When making a pitch or presentation, make sure to maintain eye contact with your audience. This can be challenging, especially if you are nervous, but it is essential for building rapport and conveying credibility.

When making eye contact, be sure to look at each person in your audience. Avoid staring at one person for too long, as this can be perceived as intimidating or aggressive. Instead, make eye contact with each person for a few seconds, then move on to the next person.

Using Gestures

Gestures are another important aspect of body language. Gestures can help to emphasise your message and make it more engaging for your audience. When using gestures, make sure to use them naturally and purposefully. Avoid using gestures that are distracting or that do not match the tone or content of your message.

When using gestures, be sure to use them at appropriate times. For example, you might use a gesture to emphasise a key point or to illustrate a concept. Avoid using gestures that are repetitive or that do not add value to your message.

Avoiding Negative Body Language

Negative body language can undermine your message and convey the wrong impression to your audience. Negative body language includes crossing your arms or legs, avoiding eye contact, slouching, or fidgeting. When making a pitch or presentation, it is important to be mindful of your body language and to avoid negative body language that can detract from your message.

Body language and nonverbal communication are essential components of any pitch or presentation. By using open body language, maintaining eye contact, using purposeful gestures, and avoiding negative body language, you can convey confidence and credibility to your audience. Remember to be mindful of your body language and to practice using open body language in everyday conversations as well as in formal presentations. By mastering these best practices, you can become a more effective communicator and convey your message with confidence and credibility.

Using Mirroring and Matching

Mirroring and matching are techniques that can help you build rapport with your audience and establish a sense of connection. Mirroring involves matching your audience's body language, tone of voice, and pace of speech. Matching involves using similar body language, tone of voice, and pace of speech as your audience.
When using mirroring and matching, it is important to be subtle and natural. Avoid mimicking your audience in a way that is obvious or contrived. Instead, use mirroring and matching to establish a sense of rapport and connection with your audience.

Using Tone of Voice

The tone of voice is another important aspect of nonverbal communication. The tone of voice can convey emotion, attitude, and intention. When making a pitch or presentation, it is important to be mindful of your tone of voice and to use it effectively to convey your message.

When using tone of voice, be sure to vary your pitch, volume, and pace. This can help to keep your audience engaged and focused on your message. Avoid using a monotone or flat tone, as this can be perceived as boring or uninteresting.

Using Pauses

Pauses are another important aspect of nonverbal communication. Pauses can be used to emphasise key points, create suspense, or give your audience time to process information. When using pauses, be sure to use them purposefully and strategically. Avoid using pauses that are too long or that detract from your message.

Using Facial Expressions

Facial expressions are an important aspect of nonverbal communication. Facial expressions can convey emotions, attitudes, and intentions. When making a pitch or presentation, be sure to use facial expressions that are appropriate to your message.

For example, if you are presenting a serious or important message, use a serious facial expression to convey the gravity of the situation. If you are presenting a lighthearted or humorous message, use a smile or a playful facial expression to convey the tone of your message.

Body language and nonverbal communication are essential components of any pitch or presentation. By using open body language, maintaining eye contact, using purposeful gestures, avoiding negative body language, using mirroring and matching, using tone of voice effectively, using pauses, and using facial expressions, you can convey confidence and credibility to your audience. Remember to be mindful of your body language and nonverbal communication and to practice using these techniques in everyday conversations as well as in formal presentations. By mastering these best practices, you can become a more effective communicator and convey your message with confidence and credibility.

CHAPTER 15: VOICE AND TONE: MASTERING THE ART OF VOCAL DELIVERY

When it comes to making a pitch or presentation, your voice and tone can have a significant impact on how your audience perceives you and your message. Your vocal delivery can convey confidence, sincerity, and enthusiasm, or it can convey uncertainty, insincerity, and disinterest. In this chapter, we will explore the best practices for mastering the art of vocal delivery and conveying your message with confidence and credibility.

The Importance of Vocal Delivery

The vocal delivery is how you use your voice to convey your message. Vocal delivery includes tone, pitch, pace, volume, and inflection. Your vocal delivery can have a significant impact on how your audience perceives you and your message. For example, if you speak too quickly or in a monotone voice, your audience may perceive you as nervous or uninterested. Conversely, if you speak with enthusiasm and inflexion, your audience will perceive you as confident and engaging.

Using Tone Effectively

The tone is one of the most important aspects of vocal delivery. Tone refers to the emotional quality of your voice. Tone can convey emotion, attitude, and intention. When making a pitch or presentation, it is important to be mindful of your tone and to use it effectively to convey your message.

When using tone, be sure to vary your tone appropriately. Use a serious tone when presenting serious or important information, and use a playful tone when presenting lighthearted or humorous information. Avoid using a monotone or flat tone, as this can be perceived as boring or uninteresting.

Using Pitch Effectively

Pitch is another important aspect of vocal delivery. Pitch refers to the highness or lowness of your voice. When using pitch, be sure to vary your pitch appropriately. Use a higher pitch to convey excitement or enthusiasm, and use a lower pitch to convey seriousness or importance.

Avoid using a pitch that is too high or too low, as this can be perceived as unnatural or forced. Instead, use pitch variations that are natural and appropriate to your message.

Using Pace Effectively

Pace is the speed at which you speak. When using pace, be sure to vary your pace appropriately. Use a slower pace when presenting important or complex information, and use a faster pace when presenting simpler or less important information.
Avoid speaking too quickly or too slowly, as this can be perceived as nervous or uninterested. Instead, use a pace that is natural and appropriate to your message.

Using Volume Effectively

Volume refers to the loudness or softness of your voice. When using volume, be sure to vary your volume appropriately. Use a louder volume to convey excitement or enthusiasm, and use a softer volume to convey seriousness or importance.
Avoid speaking too loudly or too softly, as this can be perceived as unprofessional or inappropriate. Instead, use volume variations that are natural and appropriate to your message.

Using Inflection Effectively

Inflection refers to the rise and fall of your voice. When using inflection, be sure to vary your inflection appropriately. Use inflection to emphasise key points or to create a sense of urgency or importance.
Avoid using inflection that is too exaggerated or that detracts from your message. Instead, use inflection variations that are natural and appropriate to your

message.

Using Pauses Effectively

Pauses are an important aspect of vocal delivery. Pauses can be used to emphasise key points, create suspense, or give your audience time to process information. When using pauses, be sure to use them purposefully and strategically. Avoid using pauses that are too long or that detract from your message.

Using Pronunciation and Enunciation Effectively

Pronunciation and enunciation are important aspects of vocal delivery. Pronunciation refers to how you say words, while enunciation refers to the clarity with which you articulate words. When making a pitch or presentation, it is important to be mindful of your pronunciation and enunciation and to use them effectively to convey your message.

When using pronunciation, be sure to pronounce words correctly and clearly. Avoid mispronouncing words or using slang or colloquialisms that may not be familiar to your audience.

When using enunciation, be sure to articulate words clearly and distinctly. Avoid slurring words or speaking too quickly, as this can make it difficult for your audience to understand your message.

Using Vocal Warm-Up Exercises

Before making a pitch or presentation, it is important to warm up your voice. Vocal warm-up exercises can help to prepare your voice for speaking and to improve your vocal delivery. Some effective vocal warm-up exercises include:

- Humming: Humming can help to relax your vocal cords and improve your vocal tone.
- Lip trills: Lip trills can help to improve your breath control and support your vocal delivery.
- Tongue twisters: Tongue twisters can help to improve your pronunciation and enunciation.
- Breathing exercises: Breathing exercises can help to improve your breath control and support your vocal delivery.

Using Voice Modulation Techniques

Voice modulation techniques can help to improve your vocal delivery and convey your message with confidence and credibility. Voice modulation techniques include:

- Volume modulation: Varying your volume to emphasise key points or create a sense of urgency or importance.
- Pitch modulation: Varying your pitch to convey emotion, enthusiasm, or seriousness.
- Pace modulation: Varying your pace to emphasise key points or create a sense of urgency or importance.
- Inflection modulation: Varying your inflection to emphasise key points or create a sense of urgency or importance.

Using Voice Recording and Analysis Tools

Voice recording and analysis tools can help you to

improve your vocal delivery by providing feedback on your tone, pitch, pace, volume, and inflection. Some effective voice recording and analysis tools include:

- Voice memo apps: Voice memo apps allow you to record your voice and listen back to it to evaluate your vocal delivery.
- Speech analysis software: Speech analysis software can analyse your voice recordings and provide feedback on your tone, pitch, pace, volume, and inflection.

The vocal delivery is an essential component of any pitch or presentation. By using tone, pitch, pace, volume, inflection, pronunciation, enunciation, vocal warm-up exercises, voice modulation techniques, and voice recording and analysis tools, you can improve your vocal delivery and convey your message with confidence and credibility. Remember to be mindful of your vocal delivery and to practice using these techniques in everyday conversations as well as in formal presentations. By mastering these best practices, you can become a more effective communicator and convey your message with confidence and credibility.

CHAPTER 16: HANDLING QUESTIONS AND OBJECTIONS: PREPARING FOR THE UNEXPECTED

When making a pitch or presentation, it's important to be prepared for questions and objections from your audience. Questions and objections can provide valuable feedback and insights into your message, but they can also derail your presentation if you are not prepared to handle them effectively. In this chapter, we will explore the best practices for handling questions and objections and preparing for the unexpected.

Preparing for Questions and Objections

Before making a pitch or presentation, it is important

to anticipate the questions and objections that your audience may have. This can help you to prepare your message and to address potential concerns before they are raised by your audience.

To prepare for questions and objections, consider the following:

- Know your audience: Understanding your audience and their needs can help you to anticipate their questions and objections.
- Know your message: Knowing your message and the key points you want to convey can help you to prepare responses to potential questions and objections.
- Practice: Practice your presentation and prepare responses to potential questions and objections in advance.
- Research: Research your audience and their industry to gain insights into their concerns and potential objections.

Handling Questions

When handling questions from your audience, it is important to be prepared, confident, and professional. To handle questions effectively, consider the following:

- Listen carefully: Listen carefully to the question and make sure you understand it before responding.
- Repeat the question: Repeat the question back to the audience to ensure that you have understood it correctly and to provide clarity for other audience members who may not have heard the question.
- Be concise: Be concise and to the point in your

response. Avoid going off on tangents or providing unnecessary information.

- Be honest: Be honest and transparent in your response. If you don't know the answer, say so and offer to follow up with more information.
- Stay on topic: Stay on topic and keep your response relevant to the question being asked.

Handling Objections

When handling objections from your audience, it is important to be prepared, confident, and empathetic. Objections can be challenging, but they can also provide valuable insights into your message and help you to refine your pitch. To handle objections effectively, consider the following:

- Acknowledge the objection: Acknowledge the objection and take it seriously. Avoid dismissing the objection or becoming defensive.
- Empathise with the audience member and their concerns. Try to understand their perspective and offer solutions that address their concerns.
- Address the objection: Address the objection directly and provide a clear response that addresses the concern.
- Provide evidence: Provide evidence to support your response and to reinforce the credibility of your message.
- Stay positive: Stay optimistic, even in the face of challenging objections. Remember that objections can provide valuable feedback and insights into your message.

Handling questions and objections is an essential component of any pitch or presentation. By preparing for questions and objections, listening carefully, being concise, being honest, staying on topic, acknowledging objections, empathising with the audience, addressing objections directly, providing evidence, and staying positive, you can handle questions and objections effectively and convey your message with confidence and credibility. Remember to be prepared, confident, and professional, and to view questions and objections as opportunities to refine your message and improve your pitch.

CHAPTER 17: ADAPTING TO VIRTUAL PITCHES: EMBRACING THE DIGITAL LANDSCAPE

The emergence of digital technology has transformed the way we communicate, and this is particularly evident in the world of business pitching. With the rise of remote work and online meetings, virtual pitches have become an essential part of the modern business landscape. In this chapter, we will explore the best practices for adapting to virtual pitches and embracing the digital landscape.

The Benefits of Virtual Pitches

Virtual pitches offer several benefits over traditional in-person pitches, including:

- Increased accessibility: Virtual pitches can be accessed from anywhere in the world, making it easier to connect with a wider range of potential investors, clients, or partners.
- Cost savings: Virtual pitches eliminate the need for travel and other expenses associated with in-person pitches, making them a more cost-effective option for businesses of all sizes.
- Time savings: Virtual pitches can be scheduled and conducted more efficiently than in-person pitches, saving time for both the presenter and the audience.
- Improved collaboration: Virtual pitches can facilitate collaboration and teamwork among remote team members, making it easier to work together on a shared project or goal.

Best Practices for Virtual Pitches

To ensure that your virtual pitch is effective and engaging, consider the following best practices:

- Use high-quality equipment: Use high-quality equipment, including a reliable internet connection, a high-quality webcam, and a microphone to ensure that your presentation is clear and professional.
- Choose a quiet, well-lit location: Choose a quiet, well-lit location for your presentation to avoid distractions and ensure that your audience can see and hear you.
- Test your technology: Test your technology in advance to ensure that everything is working properly and that you are familiar with the platform

you are using.

- Use visual aids: Use visual aids, such as slides or videos, to reinforce your message and make it easier for your audience to follow along.
- Engage your audience: Engage your audience by asking questions, using polls, or encouraging participation through chat or other interactive tools.
- Use nonverbal communication: Use nonverbal communication, such as hand gestures and facial expressions, to convey confidence and credibility.
- Keep it concise: Keep your presentation concise and to the point, as attention spans can be shorter during virtual presentations.
- Follow up: Follow up with your audience after the presentation to answer any questions or provide additional information.

Adapting to Virtual Presentations

Adapting to virtual presentations requires a shift in mindset and approach. To adapt to virtual presentations effectively, consider the following:

- Embrace the technology: Embrace the technology and be open to new ways of communicating and collaborating.
- Prepare in advance: Prepare in advance to ensure that you are familiar with the technology and that you have everything you need for a successful presentation.
- Be flexible: Be flexible and adaptable, as virtual presentations can present unexpected challenges or technical issues.

- Focus on engagement: Focus on engagement and interaction to ensure that your audience remains engaged and interested throughout your presentation.

Virtual pitches are an essential part of the modern business landscape, and adapting to virtual presentations is key to success in today's digital world. By using high-quality equipment, choosing a quiet and well-lit location, testing your technology, using visual aids, engaging your audience, using nonverbal communication, keeping your presentation concise, and following up with your audience, you can deliver a compelling virtual pitch. Remember to embrace the technology, prepare in advance, be flexible, and focus on engagement to ensure that your virtual presentations are successful and achieve your goals.

CHAPTER 18: REAL-LIFE EXAMPLES: INSPIRING PITCHES AND LESSONS LEARNED

Real-life examples of successful pitches can be a valuable source of inspiration and learning for pitchers. By examining successful pitches and the strategies that led to their success, pitchers can gain insights into what works and what doesn't, refine their strategies, and increase their chances of success. In this chapter, we will explore real-life examples of inspiring pitches and the lessons that can be learned from them.

Example 1: Apple's iPhone Launch

One of the most iconic and successful product launches in recent history is Apple's iPhone launch in 2007. The pitch focused on the product's innovative features, such as its touchscreen interface and built-in iPod, and emphasised the benefits to the user, such as convenience and ease of use. The pitch also highlighted the product's sleek design and emphasised its superiority over competitors.

Lessons Learned:

- Focus on benefits: Apple's pitch focused on the benefits of the product, rather than just its features, and emphasised how it would improve the user's life.
- Highlight uniqueness: Apple's pitch emphasised the uniqueness and superiority of the product over competitors, highlighting what made it different and better.
- Use visuals: Apple used visuals, such as images of the product, to support the pitch and make it more engaging.

Example 2: Uber's Pitch to Investors

Uber's pitch to investors in 2010 was focused on disrupting the transportation industry by providing a more efficient and convenient alternative to traditional taxis. The pitch highlighted the potential market size and the company's ability to scale quickly, as well as the benefits to both drivers and passengers.

Lessons Learned:

- Identify a problem to solve: Uber's pitch focused on identifying a problem in the market and providing a solution that was more efficient and convenient.
- Highlight potential market size: Uber's pitch highlighted the potential market size and the company's ability to scale quickly, demonstrating the potential for significant growth.

- Emphasise benefits to all stakeholders: Uber's pitch emphasised the benefits to both drivers and passengers, highlighting how the product would improve the lives of both groups.

Example 3: Elon Musk's SpaceX Presentation

Elon Musk's presentation on SpaceX's Mars mission was focused on the long-term vision and the potential impact of the mission on humanity. The pitch emphasised the importance of space exploration and the potential benefits to humanity, such as colonisation and ensuring the survival of the species.
Lessons Learned:

- Emphasise long-term vision: Elon Musk's pitch emphasised the long-term vision of the project and the potential impact it could have on humanity.
- Highlight potential benefits: Musk's pitch highlighted the potential benefits of the mission, such as colonisation and ensuring the survival of the species, to show why it was important and worth pursuing.
- Create a sense of urgency: Musk's pitch created a sense of urgency around the mission, emphasising the importance of acting now to ensure the survival of humanity.

Example 4: Patagonia's Environmental Pitch

Patagonia's pitch to consumers focused on the company's commitment to environmental sustainability and the impact of consumer choices on the planet. The pitch emphasised the importance of making responsible choices and highlighted the company's efforts to minimise its environmental impact.

Lessons Learned:

- Highlight company values: Patagonia's pitch highlighted the company's commitment to environmental sustainability and its values as a company.
- Emphasise the impact of consumer choices: Patagonia's pitch emphasised the impact of consumer choices on the planet and highlighted the importance of making responsible choices.
- Show actions, not just words: Patagonia's pitch highlighted the company's efforts to minimise its environmental impact, showing how it was walking the talk and not just making empty promises.

Example 5: Gener8 on Dragons Den.

Another real-life example of an inspiring pitch is the pitch made by Sam Jones, founder of Gener8, on the BBC version of Dragons' Den. Gener8 is a browser extension that allows users to earn rewards for sharing their data with advertisers. During his pitch, Jones emphasised the importance of data privacy and ownership and highlighted the potential for users to earn rewards while retaining control over their data.

Jones' pitch was successful, and he was able to secure investments from Dragons Peter Jones and Touker Suleyman, with the latter also offering free office space for a year for Gener8. The success of Jones' pitch can

be attributed to several factors, including his clear and compelling message, his emphasis on data privacy and ownership, and his ability to demonstrate the potential value of the product to both users and advertisers. He also demonstrated superb listening skills and answered each question clearly and succinctly in turn.
Lessons Learned:

- Focus on a clear and compelling message: Jones' pitch was focused on a clear and compelling message that resonated with his audience and highlighted the unique value proposition of his product.
- Emphasise the importance of data privacy and ownership: Jones' pitch emphasised the importance of data privacy and ownership, a topic that has become increasingly relevant in today's digital age.
- Demonstrate the potential value of the product: Jones' pitch demonstrated the potential value of the product to both users and advertisers, highlighting the benefits of data sharing for both parties.
- Engage the audience: Jones' pitch was engaging and interactive, using visual aids and examples to support his message and make it more memorable.

By analysing successful pitches like Jones', pitchers can gain insights into what works and what doesn't, refine their strategies, and increase their chances of success. Remember to focus on a clear and compelling message, emphasise the unique value proposition of your product, demonstrate the potential value to your audience, and engage your audience through visuals and examples.

Conclusion

Real-life examples of successful pitches can be a valuable source of inspiration and learning for pitchers. By examining successful pitches and the strategies that led to their success, pitchers can gain insights into what works and what doesn't, refine their strategies, and increase their chances of success. The examples provided in this chapter highlight the importance of focusing on benefits, uniqueness, and visuals, as well as identifying problems to solve, highlighting the potential market size and benefits to stakeholders, emphasising long-term vision and potential impact, and highlighting company values and actions.
It is important to note that while real-life examples can provide inspiration and learning, it is equally important to adopt strategies for your unique situation and audience. What works for one business or audience may not work for another, and it is important to be flexible and adaptable in your approach. Additionally, it is important to balance inspiration with practicality, focusing on strategies that are relevant and applicable to your specific situation.

To incorporate real-life examples into your pitching strategies, consider the following tips:

- Research successful pitches in your industry or niche: Look for examples of successful pitches in your industry or niche and analyse the strategies that led to their success.
- Identify what worked and what didn't: Analyse

successful pitches to identify what worked and what didn't, and use this information to refine your approach.

- Adapt strategies to your situation: Adapt strategies to your situation and audience, taking into account your unique value proposition, market, and audience.
- Balance inspiration with practicality: Focus on strategies that are both inspiring and practical, taking into account the specific challenges and opportunities of your situation.
- Test and refine: Test your strategies in real-world situations and refine them based on feedback and lessons learned.

By incorporating real-life examples into your pitching strategies, you can gain insights into what works and what doesn't, refine your approach, and increase your chances of success. Remember to research successful pitches in your industry, identify what worked and what didn't, adapt strategies to your situation, balance inspiration with practicality, and test and refine your strategies to ensure that they are effective and impactful.

CHAPTER 19: CONCLUSION: THE CONTINUOUS JOURNEY OF PITCH IMPROVEMENT

Pitching is a critical skill for business success, and it is a skill that can be improved through practice, preparation, and continuous learning. In this book, we have explored various strategies for improving your pitches, including the importance of a compelling pitch, tailoring your pitch to different stakeholders, mastering the art of brevity, capturing attention and securing funding, persuading prospects and closing deals, influencing colleagues and decision-makers, humanising your business idea, communicating your unique selling proposition, presenting numbers and metrics effectively, designing impactful slides and pitch decks, conveying confidence and credibility through body language and nonverbal communication, mastering the art of vocal delivery, preparing for the unexpected through handling questions and objections, rehearsing and refining your pitch, adapting to virtual pitches, building a pitch library, and learning from real-life examples.

While this book provides a comprehensive guide to improving your pitching skills, it is important to remember that the journey of pitch improvement is a continuous one. As you continue to refine and improve your pitches, you will encounter new challenges and opportunities that require you to adapt and learn new strategies. The key to success is to maintain a growth mindset and a commitment to continuous improvement.

To continue improving your pitching skills, consider the following strategies:

- Seek feedback: Seek feedback from colleagues, mentors, and other trusted advisors to gain insights into your strengths and areas for improvement.
- Analyse your performance: Analyse your performance in past pitches and identify areas for improvement, as well as areas where you have excelled.
- Learn from others: Learn from other successful pitchers by studying their strategies and incorporating them into your approach.
- Attend workshops and seminars: Attend workshops and seminars focused on pitching and communication to learn new strategies and stay up-to-date on industry trends.

- Practice regularly: Practice regularly to hone your skills and improve your confidence and delivery.
- Embrace new technologies: Embrace new technologies, such as virtual and augmented reality, to enhance your pitches and engage your audience.

By adopting a growth mindset and a commitment to continuous improvement, you can continue to refine and improve your pitching skills, adapt to new challenges and opportunities, and achieve greater success in your business endeavours.

Pitching is a critical skill for business success, and it is a skill that can be improved through practice, preparation, and continuous learning. In this book, we have explored various strategies for improving your pitches, including the importance of a compelling pitch, tailoring your pitch to different stakeholders, mastering the art of brevity, capturing attention and securing funding, persuading prospects and closing deals, influencing colleagues and decision-makers, humanising your business idea, communicating your unique selling proposition, presenting numbers and metrics effectively, designing impactful slides and pitch decks, conveying confidence and credibility through body language and nonverbal communication, mastering the art of vocal delivery, preparing for the unexpected through handling questions and objections, rehearsing and refining your pitch, adapting to virtual pitches, building a pitch library, and learning from real-life examples.

Remember that the journey of pitch improvement is a continuous one, and it requires a growth mindset and a commitment to continuous learning and improvement. By seeking feedback, analysing your performance, learning from others, attending workshops and seminars, practising regularly, and embracing new technologies, you can continue to refine and improve your pitching skills, adapt to new challenges and opportunities, and achieve greater success in your business endeavours.

Good luck on your journey of pitch improvement and perfecting the perfect pitch!

Matilda O'Sullivan
Ana Tagle
[illegible]
[illegible]
[illegible]
Honor Binns <3
[illegible]
[illegible]

Printed in Great Britain
by Amazon

20883538R00078